KT-210-789

Withdrawn
for sale

Ottakar's LOCAL HISTORY *Series*

Norwich

THE CASTLE.
YACHTING STATION.
THE CITY HALL FROM THE CASTLE.
NORWICH
PULLS FERRY.
CATHEDRAL.
H974

Ottakar's LOCAL HISTORY *Series*

Norwich

Compiled by Sarah Skinner,
Debbie Hockey and David F. Chapman

OTTAKAR'S

The church of St Peter Mancroft, pre-1939. The spire on the top of the tower is not original, but was added during the nineteenth century.

Front cover: *Guildhall Hill, 1919.*

Frontispiece: *Montage of Norwich, 1953.*

NORFOLK LIBRARY AND INFORMATION SERVICE

SUPP	FARR
INV. NO.	C701130
ORD DATE	13/01/03

L942.615

First published 2002

Tempus Publishing Limited
The Mill, Brimscombe Port,
Stroud, Gloucestershire, GL5 2QG

© Ottakar's plc, 2002

All rights reserved. No part of this book may be reprinted or reproduced or utilised in any form or by any electronic, mechanical or other means, now known or hereafter invented, including photocopying and recording, or in any information storage or retrieval system, without the permission in writing from the Publishers.

British Library Cataloguing in Publication Data.
A catalogue record for this book is available from the British Library.

ISBN 0 7524 2661 3

Typesetting and origination by Tempus Publishing Limited
Printed in Great Britain by Midway Colour Print, Wiltshire

Contents

Foreword 7

Note from a Newcomer to Norwich 8

1. Cherished Childhood 9

2. Working World 35

3. Wartime Wonders 44

4. Local Legends 60

5. My Norwich – A Fine City 73

6. Highdays and Holidays 101

Contributors' Biographies 121

Write Your Own Local History

Ottakar's is undertaking the most exciting local history project ever.
We are looking for the most lively and interesting
local history stories in Norwich.
We will be publishing the best pieces in an extraordinary book that will
chronicle the town's history in a unique and personal way.
If you have an interest in your town or surrounding area and would like to
have a piece of your history writing published
then this is the perfect opportunity.

Win £200

Writers of the best three pieces, according to the judges, will each win £200.
These, together with the best other pieces will be published
in a book in November 2002.

Entries will be judged locally by Ottakar's Bookstore and
by Tempus Publishing Ltd.

Submissions can be based on any of the following:
The countryside, village life, family life, school days, the war, work and
industry, farming, buildings, geography and landscape, memories of all kinds,
ghosts, myths, tradition, local characters, historical figures, sports,
the arts or a local subject of your choice.
All submissions should be factual and original work.

All submissions should be accompanied by suitable illustrations such as photographs, old postcards, drawings, letters, maps, etc. Entries may take the form of photo essays, which can include favourite family photographs.
Entries must be not less than 500 words or more than 2,500 words long.

Please send submissions to: Ottakar's Bookshop in Norwich at 11/17 Castle
Street, Norwich, Norfolk, NR2 1PB. norwich@ottakars.co.uk
by July 31st 2002.
Please see over for full terms & conditions.

OTTAKAR'S

www.ottakars.co.uk

Ottakar's competition leaflet.

Foreword

Last year, Ottakar's Bookstores in conjunction with Tempus Publishing launched the 'Local Book Project'. A series of local books with a difference: They weren't written by a group of historians, they were written by the public. Personal memories of their home town. Stories of their childhood, the war, work or personalities that had left a lasting impression on their memories. Their stories were submitted in a competition with the best articles winning money as well as seeing their memories in print.

A handful of stores throughout the Ottakar's network were selected last year, each bringing out their own volume. The response was fantastic, so when the next group of stores were selected we were delighted to discover that Norwich had been chosen to take part. This was an excellent opportunity for the Norwich store, as we haven't been in the city very long. It was a great chance to interact with the public; let them know who we are and get more involved with the community as a whole. We couldn't wait to get started!

When the management of our store on Castle Street approached me about the local book project it was with the usual 'you wouldn't mind if I put your name down for this, would you?' I'd been volunteered due to my editorial experience from previous jobs, hence my task of editing the book you are holding now. Due to the busy nature of what is a relatively new store in the city, we decided that this was not going to be a one-man job and thankfully we all agreed that a team working on this book would provide better results.

Sarah Skinner, expert on all things 'Children's book-related' was immediately recruited due to her time as a tour guide in Norwich. If anything, she did most of the work on this project, contacting just about everyone in the city about the book, sending out press releases to get the public involved, collecting all the submissions and organising the vast amounts of paperwork involved in such an undertaking. She also became hooked on collecting rare pictures and postcards of old Norwich, many of which grace this publication.

Debbie Hockey was also recruited due to her experience in publishing. When Sarah and I sat looking at the piles of paperwork, it was Debbie who managed to make sense of it all and arranged it into some printable form. Without her input, I'm sure we'd still be looking at those piles of paper today. Debbie and Sarah split the arduous task of typing up the manuscripts and hand-written entries so that we could include them – they were all so good, we didn't want to leave any out.

As for me, I moved to Norwich in 1992 to study for my degree at the Art College and just couldn't leave. I love the city, but never really found the time to find out anything about it. Working on this book has shown me a little of the amazing history of Norwich and some of the personal stories that we all have about the places where we grew up. Now is your chance to share those memories as you read this collection of everything and all things Norwich. From school antics, wartime tragedy, working graft to favourite buildings and holiday remembrances of the area.

Before you rush off to get started, we'd just like to thank a few people. First of all Tempus and Ottakar's, for giving us the opportunity to get to know Norwich a little better. To BBC Radio Norfolk, Eastern Counties Newspapers and the Millennium Library for helping to spread the word of the project and encouraging the public to get involved. To the rest of the staff at the Norwich store, for putting up with us running around like stressed maniacs as the deadlines approached. To Stephen Fry, who phoned from the set of his directorial debut in Hollywood to apologise for being unable to get an introduction to us in time, what a great guy!

But above all, thanks to all the contributors for supplying us with such a wealth of varied and amazing memories of a city that is very dear to their hearts. So that these people are not just unrecognised names in a book, we've asked each of them to supply a little biography, which can be found at the back of the book. It was incredibly hard to choose just three of these as winners and we argued extensively over which should win. In our opinion, they all deserved to, but congratulations must go to the three that we finally agreed upon: Andrew Daniels, Diane de Rees and Jenny Fox.

We hope you enjoy reading the pieces in this book as much as we have during the course of compiling it.

David F. Chapman
Ottakar's Norwich

Note From a Newcomer to Norwich

I arrived in Norwich in 1995 and instantly fell in love with the city. Two years later I trained as a tour guide and discovered all about the weird and wonderful history of Norwich. The 'obsession' continued and I started collecting pictures and postcards of the city and then researching the history behind them. The one thing that I have discovered is that George Borrow was right when he said Norwich was a 'Fine City'.

Sarah Skinner
Ottakar's Norwich

Some of Sarah Skinner's anecdotes from her time as a Norwich tour guide are included in the book and many of the pictures of old Norwich used to illustrate the text have been taken from picture postcards in her own private collection. Debbie Hockey took the pictures of Norwich today.

1 Cherished Childhood

Playplaces of our childhood

My granddaughter finds it difficult to comprehend the utter freedom we enjoyed as children in the first quarter of the last century. A builder's yard sounds like a very unlikely play-place. But so it was in our case.

In about 1900, Obadiah Hanford Rice, my grandfather, a builder with five sons, four of whom followed in the family occupation of builders and architects, bought a large tract of land to the north of the city of Norwich. It was bounded on the south by Kett's Hill, (he of the rebellion in 1549) and Plumstead Road – the highest part of the city; to the east by the lands belonging to Britannia (Infantry) Barracks and the prison; to the north by the St James' Hill edge of Mousehold Heath; and to the west by a steep, gravelly escarpment – an old pit long abandoned to the gypsies who lived there in their colourful caravans. The men made clothes pegs and the women sold them but filled us with fear and alarm. This land had all belonged to one John Moores, Freeman, once mayor of the city, shown in the records as 'gravel merchant, quarry owner

The gravel pit on Mousehold Heath where the gypsies lived, 1905.

Britannia Road in 2002, built by Obadiah Hanford Rice in 1900.

and farmer,' (was it the gravel pit where the gypsies lived?); and he had lived in the Georgian House, by this time a Nursing Home with an Edwardian façade, next door to where we lived.

The first thing my grandfather did was to build Britannia Road – two facing terraces of rather pretty, vaguely 'Arts and Crafts' houses with much woodwork about the porches, stained-glass panels in the front doors and bay windows and tiled paths to the small front gardens. It was chiefly occupied by officer's families who possibly preferred their own homes to married quarters in the barracks. In 1918 when my father was ultimately discharged from military hospital – a little disabled after being blown up on the Somme – we, my parents and I, went to live at No. 57. Then, parallel to Britannia Road, Grampa built Vincent Road. It wasn't dissimilar, but the houses were on a smaller scale. It now seems to me they were probably less expensive, probably planned for NCO's and 'other ranks'.

John Moores must have been a man of considerable substance. The farm buildings attached to his estate were of single-storey, brick and flint construction and built on two sides of a square. There were innumerable cart sheds, coach-houses, grain stores, stables, workshops and so on. From Britannia Road, two pairs of high double gates led – one, via the carriage drive at the back of the Nursing Home, (now La Siesta), to the domestic quarters; the other to the farm buildings. They enclosed between them an old orchard, known as 'Moores.'

In spite of its being relatively new and having 'all mod cons', the house my mother had really set her heart on was a little flint cottage attached to La Siesta at the end of the carriage drive. It belonged to Grampa and was empty, so in June 1919 we moved there. It had lattice windows and was of flint and brick and covered with pebbledash; its kitchen floor was of higgledy-piggledy bricks. There was no bathroom as there'd been at No. 57. This problem was soon overcome by creating one from the box-room above the hall, where a fearsome geyser was installed over the kind of bath that collectors nowadays spend a small fortune on. There was a WC with a high-up cistern, but no washbasin. An enamel bowl parked on a board over the bath did duty for that and my father's strop and shaving-mirror hung on the geyser.

The day we moved in, I stood with my maternal grandfather in the opening of a high flint wall – which was our garden gateway, with a studded oak door – looking at the milkman's donkey enjoying the thistles in the overgrown garden. The milkman, Mr

Monica Bowling, at about six years of age (left).

Senior, had a dairy in Quebec Road. I was a little short of three years old and a few weeks later my sister Pauline was born on my third birthday. Because I was now three, I went to my first school that September. It was Ardess House – one of the pretty terraced houses in Britannia Road. The proprietress and headmistress was Mrs Atthill, wife of a major from the barracks. I still remember the words and music of the action songs we learned in the sunny room at the back of the house, with its French windows opening on to the back garden... and I learnt to read.

By this time, all John Moores' farm buildings had been appropriately converted to their new uses. Heavy doors were now painted in a dullish green with their new contents in bold white lettering – Paint Store, Cement Store, Foreman's Office, Carpenter's Shop and so on. Where Moores' farm wagons had been housed, Grandfather's tumbrels were lined up in the open cart shed; and behind closed high doors, his trap and pony cart were kept. Legend has it that the day after he'd borne me to my christening, Billy the pony fell dead in the shafts and Grampa became a motorist – but that was later.

In about 1912, Grampa had the notion of making an exclusive club for Thorpe Hamlet and so the Northern Heights Sports Club was established! Two lawn tennis courts were created in the lower field and at the back of the range of cart sheds he built The Pavilion. It was the size of a small ballroom, with a pillared terrace on the west side overlooking the city. There was a small ladies' retiring-room or committee room attached, as well as outside and inside WCs and washbasins.

During its all-too-brief existence it succeeded, but the Great War intervened and when it was over, things were never the same again. This, then became the 'play place' of my childhood days. No tree was left unclimbed, no open door was unexplored and no opportunity for adventure was left unexploited. By the time I was six or seven years old, I was the magnanimous dispenser of the facilities offered by the Back Field and Moores to those less fortunate children with ordinary conventional gardens to play in. Not only that, but I was the ringleader in each and every escapade which occurred.

I have said that the carriage-drive to La Siesta led to the back of our cottage. Opposite, on the left hand side of the drive, as well as a couple of tiny cottages and the rear doors of the carpenter's shop, there stood the stables and coach house of the one-time mayor. The coach house served in turn as garage for our Triumph motorbike and sidecar, followed by our first Austin 7 in 1926. As in all similar early nineteenth-century buildings, it had a beaten earth floor and a roof of tiles laid directly on to the roof laths – with ivy poking through here and there.

But the stables! Ah, the stables! Though the carthorses had by now been long gone, the cobbled floor still had drifts of straw in the cracks; wooden pegs above each stall were where thick black horse-collars had been hung and the whole place was heavy, still, with the unforgettable smell of horse. There were two wooden mangers and a place where hay was stored. This place became our unchallenged domain.

I have said that the tiles were laid directly on to the rafters. It was simplicity itself, therefore, to move aside two or three tiles to expose a gap wide enough for a child to climb through from a standing-point on the manger, giving instant access to the roof. From here, we traversed the entire length of roofs, those overlooking the builder's yard and those overlooking the carriage-drive, via a leaded valley. Often discarding our sandals and in our bare feet, we were as agile as monkeys. By climbing up to the ridge tiles, we were masters of all we surveyed. From our cottage side, over the flint garden wall, we could see our mother in the kitchen. From

Wedding of Monica Bowling's parents in 1915.

the opposite side we could overlook the one-time farmyard, now piled high with stacks of planks, pre-formed gable-ends, rolls of wire netting, tubs, heaps of gravel, heaps of flints, in fact, everything required by a master builder in the early years of the century.

We had to exercise great caution in negotiating the hazards of roof climbing; not for fear of our skins, but for fear of being caught, chiefly by our arch-enemy, our Grandfather's foreman, Mr Ewing. He was a weasly little man with a rheumy eye and a dragglely, tobacco-stained moustache – and a fearsome temper.

There was also Mr Williams. Mr Williams was Grampa's clerk-of-works. He wore formal suits with stiff collars and had spectacles and crinkly hair. He came to work on a stately bicycle and sat on a high stool, writing in his books at a tall desk beneath the window. The office had been converted from one of the two tiny cottages between the stables and the carpenter's shop. The leaded valley between the roofs was one of the places to which we laid claim. We had a kind of 'house' up there and planted a few wild flowers in a wooden fruit tray. We also stipulated that behind a chimney stack in the middle of the lead valley was the place allocated to be our lavatory. It embarrasses me even now to write about it!

But one dreadful day there came a terrible roar from the builder's yard with Mr Ewing's voice shouting, 'Come you on down! I know you're up there. Come you on down this very minute, do I'll tell your Granfar on yer!' We peeped over the ridge tiles. He was red-faced and angry; and there was nothing for it, we had to climb down and face the music.

It seemed he had been working in the foreman's office beneath us when some telltale drops fell upon the plans spread out on his desk. In vain I feebly mendaciously protested that we'd been watering our flowerbed on the roof. I don't to this day know which of us was guilty of using the 'domestic offices' behind the chimney stack. But truth will out and we had the most awful telling off a child can have. I don't think my mother ever heard the story. She would not have been amused.

For some time after that we gave the roofs a miss and made new headquarters in the committee room behind the Pavilion, where old boxes and tea-chests did duty for furniture. And – oh, bliss – there was a little fireplace. Now that I mention the fireplace, it reminds me that we were born arsonists. Given half a chance, we lit fires, which spread excitedly in the long dry grass of summer. Huge fires, which were sometimes difficult to put out! In spite of these hazards, roofs, fires (which today would most likely expose our parents to the Health and Safety watchdogs), we none of us suffered more than the usual cuts and bruises. We behaved rather dreadfully, but not maliciously, unless you count the occasions when we made the tenants of the Kett's Hill cottages somewhat justifiably annoyed by dropping stones over the wall edging the Pavilion drive, on to the roofs of sheds and chicken houses below.

Gradually, our games changed character through the influences of the 'Silent Pictures' to which we were occasionally taken, or the books we read. When histrionics were called for, I bagged all the best parts. I remember simultaneously enacting the cruel Simon Legree and poor old Uncle Tom, staggering through the 'sugar cane' of child-high grass as we recreated Harriet Beecher Stowe's *Uncle Tom's Cabin*. I specialised in heart-rending deaths and left noble upright heroes to the others. We were fortunate that there was material at hand at the carpenter's shop to make swords and daggers from wooden laths, which we used for many games involving The Three Musketeers. cowboys and Indians were quite popular, though none of us was keen on being an Indian. The films, of course, were silent, so we had no problems inventing the words. It goes without saying, perhaps, that I wrote a play – on three of the sheets of card from a Shredded Wheat packet – in several scenes and three acts.

The time came when we outgrew Moores and the Back Field and we traversed Mousehold and went further and further afield through leafy lanes far beyond the outskirts of the city.

Monica Olwen Bowling

Wroxham village school

Moving to Hoveton-St-John from Ilford, London in 1950, was a delight. I was seven years old and my sister was four. After the rows of houses and busy streets of Ilford the country lanes seemed very empty and strange. A village, where all the roads met in the centre near the river and bridge, was so different and exciting. We were fascinated to see that all the shops were called Roy's and that the outside walls of Roy's greengrocers were painted with beautiful scenes of boats. It soon became my task to collect our Sunday paper from the newsagent, by Wroxham

Roy's of Wroxham, today.

Bridge and on every trip I'd go and stand for a few minutes in the centre of the footbridge and watch all the rowing boats, motor craft, cruisers and sailing boats.

My parents, dealing first with the practicalities of our new life, discovered that Carmans, the grocers in Wroxham had a delivery service and asked that Mr Carman call on us when next on his rounds. Wartime rationing was still being enforced in Ilford and I was used to taking the family ration books when sent on shopping errands. In the half-hopeful way that she'd developed, my mother asked wistfully if he had any eggs and showed him the family egg coupons. 'How many would you like?' he asked. 'How many can I have?' replied mother. Mr Carman tried again. 'Tell me how many you'd like?' and mother said jokingly that a dozen would be fine and was amazed when Mr Carman went out to his van and returned with a tray of one dozen. We'd been used to an allowance of two per week each. Mr Carman was a wonderfully cheerful, friendly man and delivered our weekly order, right onto the kitchen table, all the time we lived there and all the fresh farm produce was much appreciated.

The time came to attend school in Wroxham Village. The double-decker school bus stopped outside Roy's greengrocery department. Our fare was one old penny. My friend Norma Daniels collected Victorian pennies and if she'd been given one, she would dart into Roy's where her father worked, to change it for another. An old lady always travelled on the bus and got off before we reached the school – she was the only non-school passenger and I often wondered why.

Everything was such a contrast to the

modern primary school in Ilford. This little village school was built of red brick and most of the rooms lead into each other. There was even a bell hanging outside, which at one time had been used to call the village children to school. I had to become familiar with the Norfolk accent and phrasing and during the first few weeks encountered a few communication problems. For example 'You'll get wrong', but at least this was easily translated as 'You'll get into trouble.' The atmosphere and traditions of this school had been unchanged for generations. Good manners were expected and correction always given with a gentle lecture to suit the occasion. The headmaster lived in a house that was part of the school building and had a shingled area in front, instead of a real garden. The path between the girls' playground and the school entrance went past the house and one of the strictest rules was not being allowed to run there, but to walk quietly.

The girls' lavatories were on a lower level at the back of the school and visits there were known as 'going down the steps.' If one of the teachers was on the steps, we were required to wait at the top to let her pass first. As there wasn't a way through from the girls' playground, we were all marched down at suitable intervals. The outer wall of the school building seemed very high from there and I remember one very windy day when we all looked up at the building and shrieked, because it appeared to be swaying ominously. Classrooms, heated with very old-fashioned black stoves, led into one another and were divided by folding wooden doors. Therefore any child needing to 'go down the steps' had to open the screen, step into the adjacent classroom, then wait to be beckoned forward, passing between the teacher and pupils. Our desks were long benches, joined to an immovable desktop, with only a narrow shelf underneath to hold books – most inconvenient. All the teachers' desks were very high, needing a tall stool, which allowed her a good view of each child, especially as the children's desks were placed lengthways in the room, so there were only a few rows.

The classes had separate singing lessons and the sound came through the screens very clearly. I remember the class next door working on 'Cherry Ripe' and just longed to be able to sing it too and in time my class progressed to it. Mrs Woods taught us 'The Holly and the Ivy', we didn't have hymn books, but painstakingly learned by repeating, then singing one or two lines at a time. We sang this for visitors on one occasion and she reminded us which verse came next by quietly saying 'blossom,' 'berry,' 'prickle,' 'bark.' One Christmas it was announced that we were to learn a new carol, which turned out to be 'Jesus Good Above All Other'. Apparently as a class we sang 'The Lord is my Shepherd' particularly well, and when we were disbanding at the end of the school year, she asked us to sing it for her and all the teachers, for the last time.

In summer months we often left the classrooms and had lessons in The Caen Meadow and it was very pleasant sitting under the trees, seeing the river Bure winding through the fields below. We were often reminded how fortunate we were to be able to do this and to note the unusual spelling of Caen.

For the first week or so I was placed in Miss Wright's class, until Mrs Woods returned from a leave of absence. Miss Wright had a sharp brisk manner that seemed quite terrifying! I am sure she was a good teacher, but she certainly ruled by fear. She always wore a flowered overall and cycled several miles along the country lanes to school each day from the village of Salhouse, where she lived in a red brick, two-storey house on a corner. I don't remember seeing children or teachers laden with books, sports gear etc – we all just brought ourselves. The headmaster was Mr Clouting and the other teacher I remember was Miss Sandal who wore a plain blue overall. Apparently when my parents were first introduced to Mr Clouting, he said, 'I've a good name for a schoolmaster.'

The first blot, literally, came with the writing lessons. Having only learned printing with a pencil, I was suddenly in a class doing joined up writing using a dip pen and bottled ink. Too timid to do anything else, I copied the others as best I could. Being left handed was a further complication as my fist methodically smudged each word and, having produced pages of messy blotted work, I went home each day covered in ink. Miss Wright was most unsympathetic and didn't offer any clues on how to go about it. It was a great relief to be transferred to Mrs Woods' class. She had a much more gentle and kind manner of teaching. When she saw that I'd not yet learned joined-up writing, she showed me how each letter was formed with a tail to link it to the next and I gradually improved. One day I actually produced a whole page of writing without the blots and Mrs Woods held it up to show the class, saying, 'Look – you wouldn't think that Barbara did this.' There was always a great feeling of togetherness in the classes – we were all made aware of each other's progress and good efforts.

Reading was much better. At Park Hill Primary School, Ilford, I had often 'hidden' in the library corner, to escape the hated sums and quietly looked at storybooks with pictures. How it had come about I don't know, but on being tested by Mrs Woods, I found to my surprise that I could read well and was promoted to the top reading group. Reading lessons contained comprehension sections, which were sometimes confusing. Imagine a picture of some cows in a meadow, facing a large shed. My question was 'Where are the cows going?' My private reaction was 'How am I meant to know what is in the shed.' However, after due thought I announced 'The cows are going to be milked.' Wrong. The expected answer was 'The cows are going into the shed!' Mrs Woods told us that as a small girl, her nickname, given by her brothers, was 'I-read-it-in-a-book.' This was her usual reply, whenever she was asked how she knew something.

We had regular written spelling tests on word lists we had been given to memorise. These tests were taken seriously and during one session a little voice shrilled indignantly 'Please Miss, Pamela's got her spelling list hidden in her blotting paper.' Poor Pamela was made to stand before the class and asked to write on the blackboard the words called out so far, to ascertain which ones she could really spell. Cheating was never overlooked, so nobody thought ill of the child who had sneaked. And yes, it was me! Well, reading and spelling were the only things I excelled at – and this wasn't fair.

Mrs Woods used to give little homilies and I remember her once telling us that she was upset. Apparently the class had misbehaved one day and she'd been annoyed and showed it. The following day one of the little girls had said to her 'You didn't like us yesterday did you Mrs Woods, because we were naughty.' Mrs Woods assured us that she always liked us all very much, although she had been vexed with us on that occasion. 'I was most upset that you thought I didn't like you.'

It was Mrs Woods who told us, on 6 February 1952, that she had some very sad news. King George VI had died.

The next term I was old enough to return to Miss Wright. Oh dear! Her manner was always so sharp. I shall never forget the way she dealt with the boy who couldn't spell 'jumper.' In this class, spelling lessons required that a child stood alone in front of the class to be tested, which was nerve-racking in itself. After this lad had stuttered and failed, another boy was called to the front of the class. 'Spell 'jumper'' she said, which he did. The first boy still couldn't get it right. So a third boy was summoned and I still remember his fearful expression as he rose slowly to his feet – so much so that Miss Wright said 'Come on, I'm not going to hurt you.' She then made the first boy stand in the middle, whilst the other two spelled 'jumper', one into each of his ears. Again and again and again. It was meant to be a jokey way of preventing the spelling going in one ear and out the other, but the children were too young to see the humour of it. However, the boy finally learned how to spell jumper – I expect he still can! Any child who was late for school was asked to provide a really good reason. One little boy's excuse was that the alarm clock was slow and she cross-examined him unmercifully, until he was bawling, but sticking to his story of 'Sob, gulp... it was the clock, Miss, it was the clock.' On these occasions, and there were many, the rest of the class sat in silence, waiting for the storm to pass.

My problems with writing surfaced again. As I had learned how to form and join the letters, some progress was being made. However, Miss Wright now decided that being left handed was not acceptable or necessary and I was made to use the 'correct hand.' This was impossible for me and I changed back whenever I thought Miss Wright wasn't looking, but she seemed to appear from nowhere brandishing a ruler, and sternly reprimand me, firstly for using the wrong hand and secondly for disobeying her. For a few weeks I was constantly drenched in tears and smeared with ink. Oddly enough I don't remember the outcome – possibly my parents intervened, although being a stoic child, I'd not complained. However, I persevered, my writing improved and I

Wroxham – the Bure, 1927.

remained left-handed. I don't think such correction is allowed now.

At that time, eye examinations were preceded by several days of ointment being applied, to enlarge the pupils. This of course blurred one's vision so that real schoolwork was impossible. (Today quick-acting eye drops are given, followed by a reverse-action drop). The children in question were allowed

to draw instead and I enjoyed several sessions of creating patterns in coloured chalk on a large sheet of black paper. Miss Wright would not allow anyone else to even sneak a look 'You attend to your own work and let Barbara get on with hers.'

Although we were consistently disciplined, good behaviour was also remarked on and praised. One such incident I remember was Miss Wright walking round the room collecting a pencil from each desk and suddenly stopping to say 'Listen everybody, Marie had her pencil ready to hand to me – how nice to see that.' The rest of us immediately grabbed our pencils and held them aloft.

The children's feelings were always taken seriously. Just before one Remembrance Day, we'd all brought one penny to school to exchange for a poppy. The infants were given a large silky version, complete with leaves, whilst the older children had the usual small poppy. It just wasn't fair, as we'd all paid the same amount and we said so most emphatically. The headmaster was summoned and painstakingly explained that we'd all given money to help those injured in fighting for our country. We wore a poppy to show that we had given, but we didn't actually buy a poppy. Mr Clouting was willing to talk it over until he was sure that we understood and were no longer upset –which is why this small incident has stayed in my memory.

Mr Clouting occasionally arrived accompanied by men in suits – school inspectors. Mostly we knew of the visit beforehand, especially if reading progress was to be checked. The 'poor' readers had been practising a page or two of their books and sure enough, were asked to read the story. This they did, all together, with speed and accuracy. Then one of the men asked a few luckless individuals what certain single words were. Naturally they had no idea, having merely learned the story off by heart, but this was as expected, nothing was said. Some of the written work, but not mine, was inspected, with Miss Wright pointing out that 'this is a neat little girl with her hands.' At other times, Mr Clouting just popped in to the classroom for a friendly and usually informative chat. One day he asked who could think of a word ending in 'at' and the children came up with many answers, including 'oat.' 'That's a good one,' he said. Then, he told us of an easy way of finding the words. Start at the beginning of the alphabet and go through to see which letters that will fit. Oh what a good idea! It was Mr Clouting who brought the box of mugs commemorating the Coronation of Queen Elizabeth II to the classes, as issued to every child in the country – I still have mine.

I only remember one drawing and colouring lesson, although art sessions must have taken place regularly. The class had been asked each to bring a sprig of holly to copy and colour. I had sneaked my piece from a garden on the right side of the road going towards Hoveton. A huge holly bush with yellow-edged leaves, hung over a high brick wall. So, having settled down to draw our holly, we were all given one brown and one green crayon. Up went my hand 'Please Miss.' Miss Wright saw at once that I needed yellow too and issued an extra crayon. Again, this minor incident shows that although the teaching methods were regimented, our feelings were always considered.

We learned many things by rote. Apart from multiplication tables (is there another effective way to learn them?) we were always chanting something. Every morning we began with the 'twelve pence make one shilling, thirteen pence make one and a penny' ending with a triumphant 'thirty pence make half a crown.' (I still find this useful – for working out a 24-hour timetable – the train leaves at 16.00 hours. Ah ha – sixteen pence make one and four – so it is four o'clock.) We also repeated the five vowels. There was a large poster on the wall, with pictures of an apple, an egg, inkbottle, an orange and an umbrella. Miss Wright would tap twice on the apple, and on the third tap we'd all start together 'A is for Apple, E is for Egg etc.' We were very well drilled and the routine was comforting and enjoyable.

Black Beauty was the set book for one term – sometimes we read it quietly to ourselves and other times out loud. Another time we were asked to learn the 24th Psalm, which was not easy for eight year olds. After what seemed like a long period of silent reading and learning, Miss Wright tested to see what we had committed to memory. All I could remember was 'The earth is the Lord's and

Wroxham Broad, 1948.

the fullness thereof…', others managed more. She didn't chastise any of us – just praised those who had done well.

The girls had regular sewing lessons and an older child was asked to help me with my first piece of work. Another torturous lesson – this girl took it upon herself to teach me to say 'th' as well as to sew. Every few minutes she took my sewing from me and then handed it back, so that I had to say 'thank you'. Except that I said 'fank you'. 'No, thank you – "th" not "f"', she kept telling me. I tried different ways of dealing with her, by hanging on to my work, or by refusing to say thank you or fank you – I thought the lesson would never end!

Every Friday morning we listened to a schools radio broadcast – I think it was meant to be a treat. A large wooden speaker was placed on the teacher's desk and it spat out distorted speech amid crackles and buzzes. We were then thoroughly questioned on what we had just found impossible to hear. I remember one lad correctly answering a question and Miss Wright saying, 'But you were waiting outside in the hall'. 'Please Miss, I was listening through the crack of the door.' This of course proved that it was possible to hear every word clearly and actually, after a few weeks, it did seem easier. Just as well, excuses were not accepted.

Miss Wright did give little rewards. 'Smarties for smart children,' and the deserving went to her desk to receive one. She also played I Spy with us sometimes. She once chose 'S'. We just couldn't guess this and it eventually turned out to be the Shine on her desk – much too hard and almost cheating we all thought.

Any child with dirty hands and fingernails was reprimanded, although we were often given a warning that we'd have an inspection the next day. One boy was commended for having spotless hands, well-shaped and shiny nails. When questioned, he told us that the gardener had given him a manicure and buffed his nails with a powder. That was OK, but woe betide the two little girls who came to school wearing red nail varnish the following day. Having reduced them to tears of shame, Miss Wright then sent them to scrub it off with soap in the front cloakroom. Of course, she knew that this would not work, but from time to time went to see how they were progressing and to receive their cry of 'It won't come off, Miss.' Eventually she relented and produced a spirit-based remover.

Talking of the cloakroom reminds me of losing my Wellington boots. It had been impressed upon us all that we should keep the area neat and place our boots side by side under our peg. Such was the fear instilled in me that I just knew I'd fail and sure enough, the day came when I could not find my boots. Lectures and recriminations followed and my father came to deal with the situation, whereupon he spotted the one remaining pair, which I'd rejected and said in great exasperation 'Silly girl, those are yours' – I was in trouble all over again.

Miss Wright may have brandished a ruler, but she didn't often use corporal punishment – her sharp tongue was sufficient, with 'staying in at playtime' reserved for persistent bad behaviour. Even then, just before the start of the next lesson, the culprit was sent to run round the playground three times. After a while I became used to her and relaxed a little. She talked to us about out-of-school happenings sometimes. One Monday morning she related the tale of a one-legged tramp who had come begging along her road. When he had been given food and/or money and continued on his way, she happened to look out of her upstairs window. As her house was on a corner, she had a clear view of him pausing out of sight as he thought, to untie the leg he'd folded up and stride triumphantly into the distance.

Violin lessons were offered one term and a small group of children who could sing in tune were selected. I was included and weekly sessions were held in the canteen building on the other side of the road. I always waited impatiently for it to be time to leave the lesson for our music class and eventually one of the braver girls would put up her hand 'Please Miss, may the violin children go now.' Miss Wright then gave permission, once commenting 'I suppose that's what's worrying Barbara Brown'. So we trooped over to the canteen and sat in the cloakroom outside the main hall, each with a coat-peg digging into the back of our necks! The tutor was a very young man, obviously not accustomed to teaching children. Small violins, two-thirds size, were provided and we painstakingly learned the names of the strings and the basics of reading music. During the early lessons we held the violins under one arm and plucked the strings. Each week, the child who had performed the best was awarded the Violin Badge and allowed to wear it until the next week. As I did rather badly during the first two lessons, it was obvious that the teacher began to think I'd not be capable of learning. So much so that when asking each little girl in turn to play an exercise, he came to me and doubtfully asked if I wanted to try. He was most surprised when the class dunce excelled and won the coveted badge. What he didn't know was that my father is an accomplished violinist, and a little home instruction and practice had got me over the initial mysteries!

Mention of the canteen brings me to the dreaded subject of the school dinners. These were not cooked on the premises and food was chosen by its suitability to travel long distances by lorry in huge metal containers. The menu was limited and we usually dined on some sort of stew, mashed potatoes and greens, dark, strong and awful. The sweets, referred to as 'pudd'n', were usually milk pudding, i.e. rice, sago or tapioca. The last was the worst; we thought it contained staring eyes. A blob of jam in the centre was optional. Sometimes it was banana custard – this sounds better, but the bananas had been cooked in with the custard, so the sliced banana was slimy and the custard tasted funny. Needless to say, we were expected to eat everything on the plate. Drinking water was provided, in plastic beakers. These came in a variety of pale colours, plus a bright red and there was much squabbling over who had the red ones. There was a curious rule that we could only drink before the meal, between courses and at the end of the meal.

During my time at the school, some new classrooms were built on the site next to the canteen building. These were beautifully light, had modern desks and chairs. My young sister joined the infants' class there and I was very jealous that she was in the new section. It was a slightly longer walk from the school bus to her classroom and for the first few days she wailed and wanted me to accompany her, right to the door. Her teacher used to welcome her with 'Come along, Margaretta', and say 'Thank you', to me. I am sure that some people can sometimes guess what is going to happen before it does. One day I just knew that this time her teacher would put a stop to my escorting her and tell her to come alone. I tried to say goodbye as we got off the bus, but she cried, so I had to take her. As I opened the door, the teacher firmly stated that it was time to stop, using the very words that I'd been expecting. So the next day, I hardened my heart and despite more tears, left her.

Eventually my class was transferred to the new section. This playground had a white painted line where it joined the short wide drive leading down to the road. We were not allowed to cross this line and obeyed the rule implicitly. Once Mr Clouting came over to the playground of the new section, just before we lined up to march back to classes. Our teacher proudly told him that we lined ourselves up now, without being told to, he was most impressed and we felt so trusted. One day our aunt had arrived from London to visit and was waving to us from the road. Even then Margaretta and I stood with our toes on the line, unable to bring ourselves to run down to greet her. The new school buildings (since demolished and replaced by houses) somehow lacked the charm of the old school and some of the traditions were lost.

Believe it or not, I was happy during my time at the village school and what I learned proved a good basis in later years. Looking back, I can see that Miss Wright cared about us and did her duty. However, children of that age group are so ready to love and adore their class teacher and my only regret is that Miss Wright did not make this possible.

Barbara Brown

A city childhood

After about a year living in the very centre of Norwich at my grandparent's large Tudor house with our extended family, my father managed to obtain a rented house near Magdalen Gates. It was a lovely house with a parlour, three bedrooms, a bathroom and a garden back and front. We had gas fires in every room and my father had the gas lighting changed to electric. There was a piano that my father played every evening after tea. He was fond of music and had a good voice. Mother was a wonderful cook and seemed to be always in the kitchen.

I had a happy time. There were several children about my age in the neighbourhood and we played together in a lane at the back of our houses. We nearly all patronised the Saturday morning cinema show in Magdalen Street where for two pence we could enjoy the adventures of Tarzan of the Apes or Tom Mix the cowboy. We also went to the Norwich Fairs at Easter or Christmas on the old cattle market which was a mass of stalls, shooting galleries, coconut shies, round-abouts, boxing booths and huge swing boats

Agricultural Hall, pre-1914.

playing loud music being powered by steam traction engines that drove an electric dynamo. The Agriculture Hall had some super rides perhaps 'Dragons' or 'Peacocks' inside and more stalls. The noise and the smell of the engines with the crowds of people was quite something in those days as there was no television or radio for us.

A neighbouring family had a canary that had stopped singing so they decided to buy another. They asked my five-year-old brother if he would like it for a pet and gave it to my mother with the cage. The bird looked rather ragged but we decided to look after it. My grandfather used to breed canaries and he told us to feed the bird on some special seed

and my father said to my brother, 'I will get it singing for you.' He obtained an empty glass bottle and rubbed it with a wet cork. In about a week or two the bird began to sing to the squeaky sound, so the new bird and ours used to sing a duet to the entire world.

I was about ten years old when we had a test in our classroom and later I had another including an oral at another school. My father then received a letter saying that I had been selected for the City of Norwich secondary school. So in September 1925 I reported to a huge building wearing my very new bright red school cap with the Norwich City coat of arms in gold on the front and I was in my new school. I was shown to a huge central hall with hundreds of boys and then taken to my form-room. Most teachers wore gowns and the head wore a cap in the school but instead of every teacher having a cane near the blackboard and using it as in the junior school, the only person with a cane was the headmaster. To me it was a very big step in my life and I enjoyed it.

I was now a pupil at the City of Norwich School very proud in my school uniform and was now able to play football and cricket on real pitches in house games. We used to have Thursday afternoon off like most of the shops in Norwich, but we had to go to school on Saturday morning. We had loads of homework and all carried leather satchels with our workbooks as we went to the teacher in their room, science or physics lab. I was friendly with many boys in my year; one I knew was our local Gordon Camm.

When I was at the C.N.S. a very disturbing event took place. The General Strike was called in 1926 when all workers unions decided to strike in sympathy with the coal miners. This meant that all transport was affected in Britain. There were no trams so I had walk about three miles across Norwich to school as schools were not closed. All factories in Norwich were closed but shops were open, but I had to rise early and walk to school, although one morning I was given a lift along Newmarket Road riding on the running board of an open car already full, by a kind gentleman offering lifts to walkers. A friend of mine who lived on a farm in the country rode in on the pillion of his sister's motorcycle and I saw a couple of schoolboys riding into Norwich on ponies. There were no buses or trains. The Strike lasted for a week and I believe Parliament made future General Strikes illegal.

After the General Strike my father bought me a bicycle, which solved my transport problem and I was soon charging down St Stephens Street, which at the time was very narrow and had dangerous tramlines. Soon nearly every boy had a bicycle and the headmaster who drove an Austin Seven made a rule that we had to ride no more than two abreast. It was said that he did not get into his car but wrapped it round him.

One lunchtime I went with several boys to Marston Lane near Harford Bridges where we had discovered an open chalk mine and we had fun using bicycle lamps and torches exploring the tunnels. On coming to the surface we found in the daylight that we were covered with chalk, so many nice clean white handkerchiefs were left behind after the cleanup. What did our mothers think!

Sports day, the swimming gala at the old Swan Swimming Club's pool and hearing 500 voices singing the School Song on Speech Day were all wonderful and have left vivid memories.

Marston Lane was a favourite place for me. I once rode down and saw an army of frogs crossing from one side to the other. I often watched sand martins fly in and out of their nest burrows in a sand cliff on the golf course and several times I saw the flash of a kingfisher over a stream. I once spent a few days at a schoolfriend's farm where I helped picking potatoes and enjoyed the ride back home sitting sideways on the broad back of a huge and gentle farm horse, all things that made me love the countryside.

Raymond Vincent
(submitted by Peter Chenery)

Argyle Street in the 1950s
Prize-winning entry

Sometime in 1952, my father negotiated the steepness of Southgate Lane with a handcart on which were gathered some, though surely not all, his and my mother's possessions. We were moving to a council house in Argyle Street and somewhere amongst it all was me, aged three. The event is my earliest memory. The setting down of childhood memories is not something to be undertaken lightly. Recollections, particularly early ones, suffer an unconscious process of selection and as a result may lack the context needed for an accurate picture – anecdotal streams often refresh the writer more than the reader. There is also a more personal, almost metaphysical, concern. Writing changes things. History becomes what its interpreters make it out to be and this is also true of individuals and their memories. Could mine, once described, cease to be the mental images they have always been and become instead only the words I have chosen to describe them? Alternatively, perhaps one should get them out of one's system... youthful urban warrior turned ageing urban worrier.

The reader may wonder whether such an exercise can be said to constitute 'History' at all. That depends on what he or she means by the term; opinions vary, especially amongst historians. Is history 'more or less bunk', as Henry Ford claimed, or an indispensable guide to the future? Is Andrew Daniels of Argyle Street as relevant as Henry Tudor of Hampton Court? Possibly not, but the modern view allows that he may at least contribute in some small, less regal way – by blowing off dust, perhaps, in history's bargain basement. Events described here are, after all, 'half a century' away and set against a backdrop that has either changed immeasurably or simply disappeared.

In the 1950s, the upward sweep from

Andrew Daniels.

Argyle Street 'to the city', an area squeezed between Ber Street and King Street, was characterised by tight patterns of narrow, often steep, streets, all lined with terraced houses which even then were at least seventy years old. Most are long gone: Compass Street, Arthur Street, Burleigh Street, St Bartholomew Street, and St Julian Street. Those that remain, Mariners Lane, Horns Lane, and Thorn Lane, do so only as partial and unrecognisable tokens of their previous existence, bisected as they now are by the 1970s spaciousness of Rouen Road. Ironically, for this really is local history, the 1950s maps of the area previously held by Norwich Central Library were lost in the fire which destroyed it. The map used here dates from 1907 – things changed more slowly in the old days. The repetition of small dwellings was alleviated only by the churches of Mother Julian and St Ethelreda, by the tiny infant and junior schools I attended and by a couple of patches of overgrown waste-ground. One of these, I have discovered, was the site of a malthouse, one of several which formerly supported the King Street breweries. In my day these were Steward and Patterson and Youngs and Crawshay and the irresistible smell of their processing was one I grew up with. The open doors of summer-time pubs (King Street was particularly well supplied) also provided a growing boy with hoppy whiffs of future pleasures. This harmless and unlooked-for

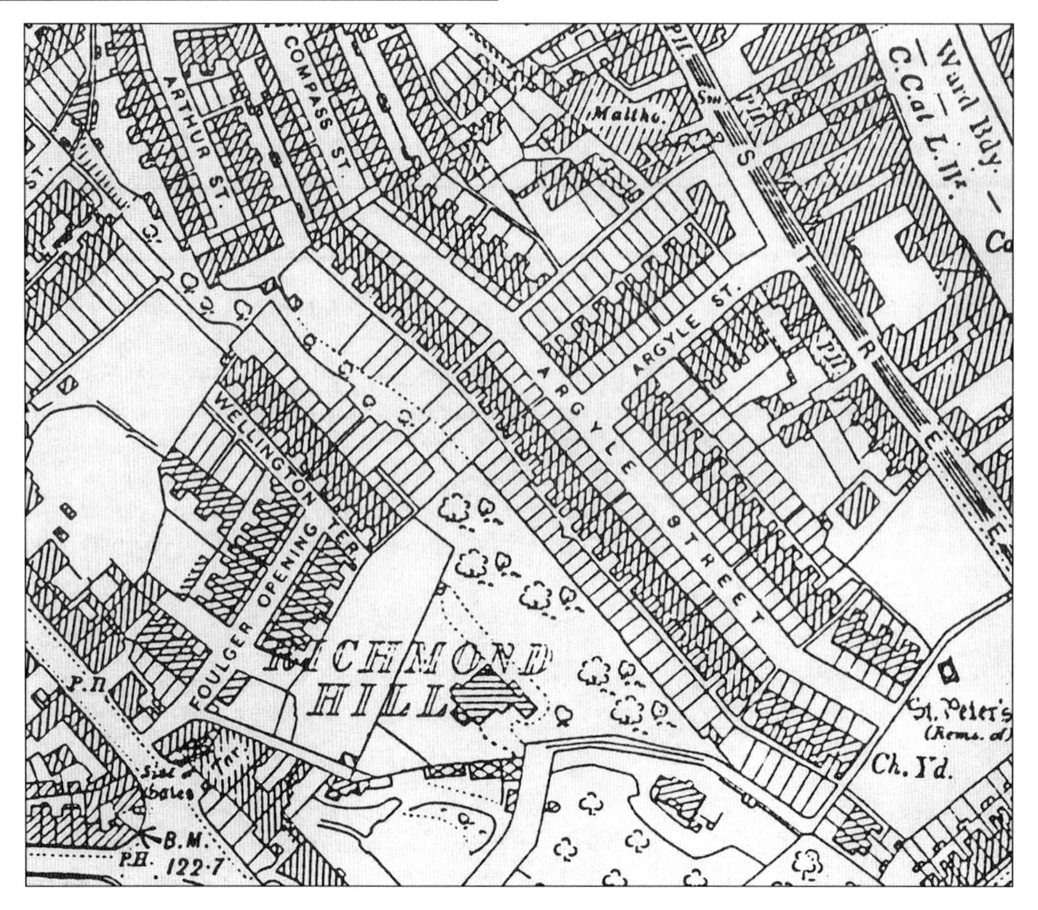

Map of Argyle Street, c. 1907.

experience was no doubt responsible for the many pints of Watney's Red Barrel I consumed in the subsequent decade.

The Argyle Street end of this wasteland, 'over the dump', was the venue for the annual bonfire, built and dismantled, re-built and dismantled, over many pre-November weeks and constructed from anything that would burn and which could be begged, borrowed and occasionally, stolen. Fireworks, at least in my case, were bought individually from Strivens' shop in Ber Street over a similar period, kept in a box and endlessly brought out for inspection on the rug before the living-room fire. I realise only now that more gunpowder lay ominously within its knitted tassles than ice lay in wait for a certain ship and more, certainly, than remained in the fireworks themselves. This is no doubt why, when 5 November finally arrived, I suffered no accidents. In those days, anyone not holding fireworks, including 'bangers', whilst lighting them was likely to be taunted and what happened to them after lighting is a subject best left undiscussed. Modern displays are safer and more spectacular, if less thrilling.

The lower, more verdant end of the 'dump' was perfect for games of 'Commandos', 'Cowboys and Indians' or 'Robin Hood'. For the latter, we made bows and arrows from branches and cut decorative strips from their bark with penknives (older, more 'dubious' boys had sheath knives). On one occasion, a map hastily scribbled on a page torn from an exercise book was sufficient, when 'discovered' in a bush, to persuade the more innocent that Crusaders had passed through Argyle Street on their way to the Holy Land. The nature of such games depended on the most recent sixpenny offering at the Regent, Norvic or Gaumont cinemas on a Saturday morning. If the commissionaire could be successfully distracted, one 'legitimate' entrant could open the fire exit for several others, although the Norvic's man was particularly fearsome and occasionally we were ejected. Once in and relatively settled, we enjoyed a cartoon, an episode of the serial (perhaps *Batman* or *Roy Rogers*) and a feature. Often this was a fairly gentle adventure from the Children's Film Foundation, but occasionally a swashbuckler turned up and an hour later several scruffy buccaneers would sword fight noisily, though without resolution, fatalities, or indeed swords, along Ber Street, down Mariners Lane to Argyle Street and dinner. (For 'dinner', read 'lunch': only 'posh' people had dinner in the evenings.)

At the top of the street was St Peter's churchyard, whose perimeter wall ran steeply down one side of Southgate Lane. The church itself, shown as intact on an 1880 map, but only as 'Rems. of' by 1907, was no more than a pile of flinty rubble in the 1950s, but the churchyard itself was the other waste-ground haunt of Argyle Street boys. There was something more edgy, somehow, about being 'over the Chuchy.' This was partly due to its associations, but also to the height of the wall from Southgate Lane, higher still from King Street. Only when slightly older and more agile could one scale it and become unavailable and I see now that activities there were perhaps a little less innocent; it was where one 'got up to things'. Even so, one harmless game bears the telling. On match days at Carrow Road, supporters poured down Southgate Lane on their way to the football ground, their adult heads below the top of the churchyard wall. One of the 'chuchy's' secrets, however, was that the ground level on the other side was several feet higher and it was possible to pour collected berries into the brims of trilbys – essential attire for respectable 1950s men. These, to much stifled amusement from above, would rotate in an incongruous 'wall of death', only to fall sometime later, perhaps during the celebration of a Canary goal. The phrase 'hat-trick' comes to mind – fifty years too late!

A more spontaneous 'footy'-based thrill was the crushing underfoot of stink bombs during the shuffling, shoulder-to-shoulder exit of 30,000 fans from Carrow Road. To the culprits, the captive groans outweighed the personal distress; one must always be prepared to suffer in a cause! Football matches were an integral part of the 'perfect' Saturday, every small boy's favourite day, sandwiched as they were between morning cinema and evening fish and chips. Eventually, the 'flicks' was overtaken by a job delivering meat on Swapman the butcher's trade-bike. Sometimes ketchup-covered crisps stood in for fish and chips. But my keenest Saturday memory is of sitting on the front step early in the morning, when two events were likely to coincide. I would be reading the *Eagle* and the *Topper* (the first passed on to me, the second bought by my father on his way home from Boulton and Paul) when a growing din would presage the arrival at the top of the street of cattle on their way to market in the city. Comics temporarily discarded, I would watch them driven past me by stick-wielding men, human curses vying with bovine lowing. Sometimes a beast more adventurous or more stupid than the rest would venture, with steamy breath and salivary strings, into an ungated front garden, only to receive the 'thwack' of a driver's stick and a hard stare from a face behind a curtain. Eventually, the commotion would subside, peace would prevail and I would turn again to Dan Dare or Mickey the Monkey.

Behind the front step at 115 Argyle Street, events were, inevitably, more mundane. Early on, my mother bathed me in the kitchen sink with a lighted cigarette lodged immovably between her lips, its slowly lengthening ash defying gravity. Even now, at eighty-seven, she operates best thus equipped, but combinations of water and smoke still challenge my breathing. We had (ironically) a cat called Smokey. A later memory is of climbing onto a table, from where I could see myself in the mirror and miming to early pop songs on the wireless – was the programme *Easybeat*?

At Christmas time we moved from the 'living' room into the 'front' room. Presents appeared in a pillowcase, a habit I find embarrassingly difficult to abandon. From the back yard, in the middle of the night, my father once threw snowballs at unseen owls in the woods behind the house. They were keeping me awake, though there were other reasons for insomnia. In the snug fastness of the middle bedroom I was first invaded by the realisation that, if everyone had to die, this included me. I was assured by my father that this was not something for a six-year-old to worry about, but that particular invader, having gained a foothold, is never quite routed. It was soon after that; I realise now, that my father unexpectedly died. He had gone, I was told, 'to live with Jesus'. I cannot say whether the idea consoled me, for strangely, this is my only memory of the event. It may indeed have been my only knowledge of it, for in those days it was deemed unwise to involve children in such matters. I have no recollection of anyone's expressed emotion at my father's death. Is this a memory which my brain won't select, or did the mourning take place without my knowledge?

Three years previously, school life had begun. It seems I could already read, but I am at a loss to know how such a miracle could have occurred. Initially, my mother took me on the three street walk to Horns Lane Infants, usually finding on her return that I had followed quietly behind. Only then, when led unrelentingly back again, did wails of anxiety and protest ensue. In fact, I had nothing to fear and much to gain, for this was a thoughtful, kindly place, then under the wise leadership of Miss Armes. I recall teachers named Miss Ritches and Miss Glaze; I'm sure they cannot all have been 'Miss'. Like everyone else, I had a daily bottle of milk, suffered an enforced lay down after lunch and copied from the blackboard: 'Andrew has brought us a spring crocus for the nature table.' This cannot, even then, have enhanced my standing as an Argyle Street boy. Much more in keeping was my disgust at being denied the playground just when it was most worthwhile – in the snow and ice.

Later, having crossed the road to Horns Lane Junior, I was naively persuaded that a certain teacher was ever happy to be bombarded with snowballs as she arrived for school. In the event, many hands made snowballs – only one propelled them! Around this time a snowy Southgate Lane was painstakingly transformed into the longest, steepest, glassiest 'slide' in Norwich. Looking back, it seems inevitable that the elderly Argyle Street ladies who climbed it to the shops each day came down quicker than they went up. Most, indeed, surely came down even as they went up.

Remarkably, Horns Lane Junior still stands. Its hall a workshop, the classrooms where Messrs Langham and Greenwood ruled now the domain of motor mechanics. Like the Infants, this too was a friendly, intimate place; its teachers genuinely concerned to both teach and guide. Miss

Thomas, the headmistress, was perhaps more feared than Miss Armes had been. In the end I, and one or two others, had cause to be grateful to both, for both professed to recognise a 'spark' which they did all they could to promote. This was no doubt a frustrating exercise, for at that time those at the wrong end of the social scale were reluctant to capitalise on unexpected assets.

Sitting the 'eleven-plus' was, even if we did not realise it, a crossing of the Rubicon. Regardless of the results, we would all be obliged to move out of our enclosed world and be subject to other influences and temptations. On my thirteenth birthday, my mother re-married and I moved elsewhere. I was sorry to leave; sorry things had to change. These two tiny, lively schools reflected exactly the society they served. It was an area which seems, in retrospect, to have had an imaginary city wall of its own and within it a code by which its people were both proud of their diversity and united by their difficulties. As with the schools, its limitations were its strengths. Is this the essence of 'community'? Change is in the nature of things, the loss of mere bricks and mortar not something to mourn. For most, quality of life has improved greatly in fifty years. If, however, as future histories seem likely to attest, we are more isolated in our affluence, it may be because we have somehow failed to carry with us to our new developments and shopping precincts this enlivening 'spirit of place'.

The constraints imposed on this basement 'rummage' mean that much remains covered in dust: neighbourhood 'characters', many of them severely limited by ancestry, circumstance and often drink; corner shops that supplied home-made penny ice lollies along with 2oz of cheese or a single egg; a pitchless school football team that never won a game – and not least, girls. It may have seemed that only mischievous males inhabited this world, but this was not so. Even pre-teenage, pre-pubescent boys had romantic nonpareils. I still remember the names of those that I aspired to, but there are some secrets that must be kept.

Andrew Daniels

A village childhood

At the age of three I moved into '5 The Croft' in Great Melton, a newly-built council house with a very large garden. Previously we had lived at 'The Willows', a brick round Prefab and before that with my grandparents at 'The Lodge'.

I can remember picking wild flowers in the orchard for my mother and that the next door neighbour's son thought it was 'too sissy.' I can also remember helping my father in the garden, when I got old enough. One

Sandra Massen's council house at No. 5, The Croft, c. 1950.

Laying the driveway at No. 5 The Croft.

memory stands out: when he decided to lay a concrete driveway when I was about fourteen. He asked me if I knew how to mix cement and naïvely I said 'no.' He showed me how to do the first barrow load and after umpteen others I knew how!

School at the age of five was The British School – why this was its name I have no idea. Then at seven it was all change as this school closed and I moved to the National School. Both of these were in Hethersett, which in winter during heavy snow meant walking in top of the hedgerows to get there, otherwise I cycled.

At eleven I went on to Wymondham Girl's School where I was among the first pupils to attend this newly built school. To get there I had to bike to Hethersett in order to catch the bus into Wymondham. It never worried me biking down the country roads with no streetlights but just fields either side. As the bus service to Great Melton was almost non-existent the services of Miss Chrissie Hipperson were called upon if a trip to the dentist/doctor/hospital became necessary. In her big black car you felt like a queen, but of course you had to pay!

The phone box was a lifeline as not many people had a 'phone in their houses. In those days it was one penny to make a call and you had to push 'button A' to get through and then 'button B' to get your money back if you hadn't been connected. This fascinated me as I thought every time I pushed the button money would appear! The post office was situated down a long path and then within the front room of this lady's house. I was often sent to get a postal order for mum and

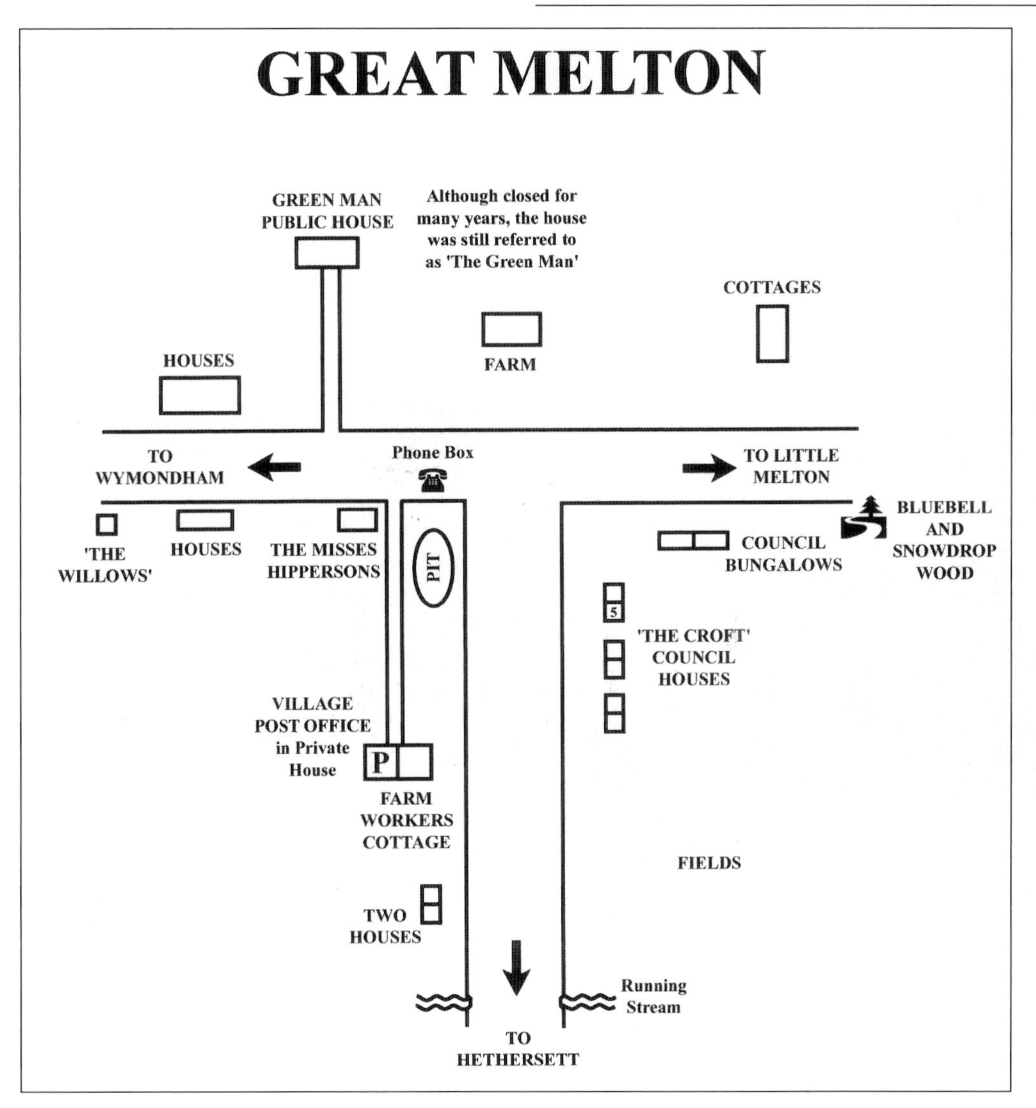

Map of Great Melton by Sandra Massen.

if the truth were known I was a bit afraid of this formidable lady.

Once a week mum's grocery order would come from Hethersett and at the same time the order for next week would be sent back with the driver. When I got older it was my Saturday morning job to take this list into the shop and collect anything that mum might have forgotten. The bread was delivered every other day, the milk daily and the coal fortnightly.

When dad used to sweep the chimney I was the one who would yell, 'the brush is out'. Mum always hated this job being done, as however hard she tried to cover the furniture etc. up dad would manage to get the soot everywhere. We did have a chimney fire once and the fire brigade had to come. This was a real treat as far as I was concerned.

At this time dad was a farmworker and a summer treat was being allowed to go and have tea with him on the field. Dad always had a bottle of cold tea to drink as this was considered to be the best thirst quencher of all. The tractor and the binder were busy and we were told to stay at the edge of the field as the binder was very dangerous – a fact that was brought home to us all when one of my friends got caught in one and died.

I lived in Melton until I married and then we moved to Norwich. This was quite a culture shock in some ways – there were buses, streetlights and shops! I still miss the changing of the season though, spring, summer and autumn – but not winter!

Sandra Massen

Sandra Massen at around eight years old.

2 Working World

Building blocks of the past

Sometimes the 'good old days' seem such a long time ago and at other times just like yesterday. I was born in 1919 and my parents lived in a cottage down a lane in a Norfolk village. We had no drinking water other than that obtained from a pond further down the lane and this would be covered with green slime in summer. The 'privy' was up the yard as were the bakehouse and washhouse. Some planning in those days!

My father was demobbed after the First World War and went back to work on the farm where he had been employed before entering the army. The wages for 'clodhoppers' were very low and after a few months he asked the farmer if he didn't think he was worth another shilling a week. Being told that if he was not satisfied he could leave on Saturday, he did so. He went to work for my grandfather who leased Hedenham Brickyard and the farm from the Ditchingham Hall estate. His main work was on the farm and at other times helping in the brickyard. As we lived in an adjoining village he walked the mile, or mile and a half, morning and night. As I have said we had no proper drinking water. Our cottage belonged to a private landlord. All the nearby cottages

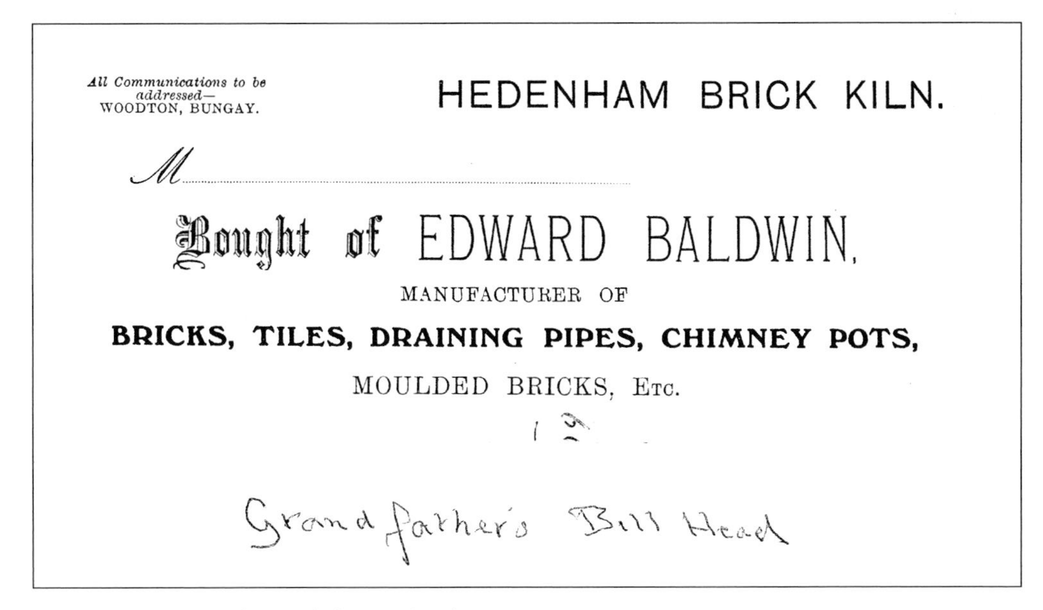

All Communications to be addressed—
WOODTON, BUNGAY.

HEDENHAM BRICK KILN.

M..

Bought of EDWARD BALDWIN,

MANUFACTURER OF

BRICKS, TILES, DRAINING PIPES, CHIMNEY POTS,

MOULDED BRICKS, ETC.

Grandfather's Bill Head

An advertising billhead from Hedenham Brick Kiln.

Hedenham Brickyard where bricks, tiles and drainpipes were made until 1935.

were part of another estate and water for them was provided from a nearby well. Dad purchased a small churn and then had to carry this filled with water home from the brickyard every evening.

At the age of three we moved to one of my grandfather's cottages in the next village. Here we were able to obtain water from a communal pump shared with the other cottages. The brickyard from before the First World War until about 1935 was a small hive of industry. Situated on what is now the B1332 Bungay to Norwich road and halfway between Hedenham and Woodton. All that remains now is the tall house where the kiln foreman lived, now a private building, and a few dilapidated buildings. The clay or 'earth' as it was called was dug out from a nearby meadow and carted by horse and tumbrel to the yard. Here the various processes were carried out, washing and milling, etc. The clay finished up with the consistency of plasticine. Power was provided by the horse walking round and round. Each brick was made individually by hand. Each man had his own 'shack' in which was a bench at which he worked. A heap of clay was placed on the bench, the clay was then put in a mould and the surplus removed, then the mould pressed down on to a base with a raised piece which would leave the impression in the base of the brick called the 'frog'. Removed from the mould, the brick would be sprinkled with fine sand and placed on a barrow standing outside the shack. When fully loaded a horse would be brought along and the bricks taken to the

'drying sheds'. These were open-sided and the bricks would remain here until ready to be transferred to the kiln. Tiles and pipes were also made, the latter by a hand-operated machine.

All this is what I remember from my childhood. I don't think that there were more than six men making the bricks. We children used to ride on the empty barrows and sometimes on the horses. No inspectors or factory Acts to 'protect' us in those far off days – I don't remember anyone getting hurt.

When enough bricks had been produced to fill the kiln, they were positioned according to the type and colour. Coal for the kiln would be fetched from Ditchingham railway station by horse and wagon. The foreman, who lived with his family in the tall house near to the kiln, would supervise the 'burning' which would take several days. He would have to be in attendance during the night to keep the fires burning. When finished and allowed to cool down, the bricks would be removed and stacked by hand, ready to be sold to various builders or used by grandfather who was also a master builder and built many houses locally. I don't know how much the brickmakers earned; it was piecework I believe. The following are some figures that I obtained some years ago from some old family account books:

Jan 26	1,000 grey books (seconds)	£4 10s 0d
Jan 30	425 Red Pantiles	£5 17s 0d
Feb 10	3 ft Drain Pipes	£5 0s 0d
Feb 10	2 Eye Pipes	£0 2s 0d
Feb 14	1,000 Inside Bricks	£3 10s 0d
Feb 14	500 Best Red Bricks	£2 10s 0d

There were many small brickyards dotted about Norfolk before the advent of the large brick making plants at Peterborough, which sounded the death knell of the small local ones.

I don't think that grandfather ever went to school. He could not write but could read. His notebook consisted of pencilled markings, which he made on pieces of wood and laid on the floor of his cart. Grandmother did the accounts and attended to all the correspondence, besides running the Primitive Methodist Sunday school, entertaining local preachers on Sunday as well as bringing up ten children.

My father worked most of the time on the farm; grandfather still used the old-fashioned methods. He had only horses for harvest, he had no self-binder, only an old-fashioned reaper or 'Sailer' as they were called. The cut corn fell onto a platform from where it was swept off by the sails on to the ground behind. It then had to be tied up by hand before being stood up in stooks. These were

Harvest time on the Brickyard Farm.

carted by horse and tumbrel or wagon to the stackyard to wait the threshing tackle later in the year. Grandfather finished both farming and brick making in 1935 and concentrated on building work.

The yesteryear I recall is gone forever. Bricks are delivered in packs and unloaded by crane, not thrown to the man standing below two at a time, caught and stacked on the site. Large tractors with multi-furrowed ploughs plough the large fields from which the hedges and ditches have been removed. Combines harvest the corn and the farming equipment rests in the museums to be looked and wondered at by visitors on Sunday afternoons. What would some of our ancestors say if they could have seen what takes place today? When an uncle of mine first had electricity laid on, an old gentleman in the cottage opposite him said 'I thought I saw some electric smoke coming out of your chimney.'

Wesley Bullen

A working city through young eyes

As a child, Norwich was to me a very interesting place, there were electric tramcars that went to all parts of the city with open tops. The fares were cheap, so it was quick and easy to move around. It had a provision market, where it is at present, with the police station at the back known locally as the 'Tin Hut' for that is what it was. The Guildhall was the Law Court, complete with cells. There were several large shops, one a jeweller, where a grand looking lady wearing a long velvet dress, lots of jewellery and beautiful white hair met you at the door. She would escort you to the counter you required and introduce you to an assistant who would serve you. My mother said she was a floorwalker in another shop that sold clothes. When you bought something, the money was put into a hollow wooden ball with a bill

The Guild Hall, post-Second World War. Postcard supplied by Sarah Skinner.

placed in some apparatus. It was pulled to the ceiling and it ran along a railway to the office that returned it by rail, containing a receipt and the change. The assistant unscrewed the ball and handed it to you.

There was a large cattle market near the castle. The cattle were driven in herds on foot along the roads to the cattle market, then after the sales, along the roads again to their destination, many going along King Street to Trowse railway station. One Saturday a bullock broke away from a herd being driven along St Benedict's Street, dashed up St Gregory's Alley, under the archway into my grandmother's open back door and promptly became jammed. Two drovers came through her front door to drive it out.

I remember going to my first football match with my father, walking through the Cathedral Close down to 'Pull's Ferry.' Being taken across the river by the ferryman at the cost of a penny each and walking to The Nest where Norwich City Football Club were playing on Rosary Road. I have forgotten the result!

What has happened to the whistling butcher boy riding his trade bike? Where are the building workers who were always singing the latest songs as they played their various skills in their work? You could tell the occupation of many people by their dress. If you saw a man wearing highly polished leather leggings above his boots called 'buskins' in Norwich on a Saturday, he was surely a farmer or smallholder. If you saw another wearing a bowler hat and spats over his shoes he could be a clerk. Most men

Pull's Ferry before reconstruction in 1949.

digging holes in the roads wore corduroy trousers with string tied round their ankles. Butchers wore blue and white striped aprons and a white boater on their heads. The baker wore a white apron as he delivered you various shapes and sizes of loaves for your choice in a covered basket. The milkman pushed a three-wheeled trolley with a large metal churn from which he filled your basin or jug using a metal measure. The policemen walked on their beat in the city but the county police had black bicycles. Schoolboys wore shorts till they left school when they 'grew up' at about fourteen and smoked cigarettes and wore long trousers.

There were some unusual trades in Norwich. I have seen men pushing trolleys of clay on rails up a yard known as 'Pipe Burners

Yard' to where there were kilns where clay pipes were made. There was also a cigarette factory near and we used to watch the men working. My paternal grandfather was known as a 'garret master', employing about four or five men making ladies shoes, very often for the larger factories. He also bred canaries for mine workers in an aviary in his back bedroom. My other grandfather was a 'master French polisher' and seemed to me always working. His workshop had a lovely smell of polish and turps and I loved watching him. At night I have seen him working with two candles sometimes wearing two pairs of spectacles one on top of the other – no wonder he went blind in old age – but a piano polished by him was a real work of art.

In the fishing ports of Lowestoft or Yarmouth many fishermen wore gold earrings and walked with a kind of roll as if they were in step with the waves. One man used to walk round the roads of Norwich with a huge wicker basket balanced on his head, shouting 'Fresh Boiled Yarmouth Shrimps!' and he would serve you with a pint of pink shrimps. Another man we called 'Charlie Oil Oil' carried a gallon can of paraffin in one hand and a metal funnel and measure in the other. Another man used to come to the back door with a large suitcase in which were reels of cotton, sewing needles, lace and buttons of all sizes and colours. My mother always seemed to need something from him. I remember while at my grandmother's there was a knock on her back door and when she answered it there was a tramp known as 'Harry Sawdust' there. She happened to have a big piece of rancid cheese in her hand that she was about to put in the bin. She asked if he wanted it and he took it and he used to call about every three months and ask if she had any more.

Of course, everyone knew 'Billy Bluelight' who used to run along the river bank alongside a pleasure boat called *The Doris* that took passengers from Foundry Bridge to Brundall Gardens before there was a railway station built there. They have named a public house after him in Hall Road in Norwich.

Raymond Vincent
(submitted by Peter Chenery)

Riverside Road, where Billy Bluelight ran his ferry, 1910.

Bonds and bombs

Thinking of Norwich in years gone by, I remember my Mother and I always went to Norwich by train, to shop at Bonds for my gymslips and clothes. I always enjoyed the day out, as there were so many shops to visit. The top of St Stephen's had a railway crossing, I think in those days it was just for freight. Bunting's had a small post office inside their shop. It was here that I opened my first saving's account, my wages were 28s 0d a month, all found.

Deacon's restaurant was on the bottom corner of St Stephen's, opposite where a policeman stood on a box directing traffic. Also in St Stephen's were Jays Furniture and Peacocks, where I bought my first suitcase, the shop opposite, which was bombed during the war and many other shops whose names escape me.

I was working at the Norfolk and Norwich Hospital in 1939. The Sunday when war was declared, us girls were having our mid-morning break when Neville Chamberlain said our country was at war. The first bombs fell on Norwich 9 July 1940, hitting Barnard's factory at Mousehold, Colman's Carrow works and Boulton and Paul's loco sheds at Thorpe station. Several people were killed and lots were injured. When the sirens sounded at night we spent several hours in the shelter until the all clear went. There was always the blackout.

When I travelled home to see my parents by train, there was a blue light in the carriages, no signs on the platforms at night and one would listen for the porter to call the name of the station. I also remember a Stephen's Rocket in a case; you put a 1d in and it worked, but is no longer there at the

Evelyn Knights, aged twenty-one, in 1944.

station. I must not forget to mention the Hippodrome at 9d, when we could afford it, and the Haymarket cinema.

I still enjoy my visits to Norwich, although they are few and far between these days. Where have all the years gone?

Evelyn Knights

City hall

It was during the 1930s that one of Norwich's largest and most imposing buildings went up – the City Hall. It was designed to look like a Scandinavian municipal building, but reflects the era's interest in Egyptology as the main doorway is guarded by Abyssinian Lions. The building wasn't popular with the locals however, as they nicknamed it 'The Marmalade Factory' on account of the garish orange brick colour.

Sarah Skinner

A side view of the City Hall.

3 Wartime Wonders

Hilda's war

Hilda was born in Norwich where she has lived all her life and is in her eightieth year. As small children growing up together in a one-bedroomed house, at bedtime her two brothers slept at the top of the bed and Hilda and her sister at the bottom of the same bed. Their parents slept over the other side of the same room. All they had for lighting was a gas mantle that had sticky flypaper hanging from it, and the five houses shared two toilets.

They spent most of their time down by the old Dolphin Bridge, either swimming, boating or fishing. The Dolphin pub, 'an exceptionally nice little pub, had everything there; all kinds of birds and animals, great big lawns, cages running round the gardens. They had geese. They had peacocks. They had goats. Ooh, they had one old goat called Billy. He used to be on the meadow as you crossed the Dolphin Bridge and he was as good as any guard dog 'cos he'd make a run for the big railings and he'd batter them with his head'. Hilda's brother Sid and that goat waged a war of nerves over a series of hot summers. 'The beast got upset and thundered towards us and those big metal railings and as he hit it my brother grabbed his horns and shook his head. You can see the dent in the railings now... '.

When she was six, they went to Mace's Buildings, moving in with her grandfather, along Heigham Street towards Mile Cross Mansion and near the Eagle Park, 'so we didn't have to go any farther for entertainment and we spent the rest of our lives down there... '.

In her teens when the war started, one of Hilda's jobs was with Chamberlin's in Botolph Street. 'Well, that was lovely, but that weren't much pay. You had to work on your own time by how many you turned out in an hour. And that was a farthing for a waistcoat, 2d for a blouse, battle blouse, 3d for a pair of army trousers, 4d for a big army topcoat. That was a lot of work. We were making those and we were making demob suits which were the same price.' The girls worked through their dinner hour to try to make the money up but considered themselves lucky with three pounds at the end of the week. 'It takes a lot of waistcoats at a farthing a time to make any money... '.

Hilda worked for a time at Caley's chocolate factory whilst Seimens took space to make batteries for the army. The machinery was always getting blocked. 'So you'd go down to the engineers' shop and say "Can I have a big spanner?" He'd say, "You can't do that." I'd say, "Yes I can." He'd say, "I can't spare anyone to come down". I said, "I can do it if you give it to me." I used to take it all off and clean it all down and put it all back... I did a lot and enjoyed every minute of the time. I'm not saying I enjoyed the bombing and raiding and that. I can honestly say I'm more afraid of a storm now than I was in wartime... You could hear the bombs that had nobody in them; you knew they were being propelled across. You knew when the engine cut out they were going to come down... '.

They would hear the barrage balloons wound up in the fields and know there was going to be a raid. Her father, a voluntary air-raid warden, said to her one night, 'It's going to be a close one'. Hilda would never go down the shelter alone; she couldn't bear being in it and used to stand outside even knowing it was going to be a 'close one'. 'And it was a close one; that hit on the corner of Old Palace Road. There was a surface shelter there and Dad said, "It's not finished yet". And then they dropped a load! Well they dropped a blast bomb on Old Palace Road.' She and her father went to look. 'Dad said, "Don't you come". I said, "I want to come. I want to see what's happened". He said, "No, you're not coming down because I think I know what's happened on the corner". He said, "I don't want you to see that". Near the surface shelter was a little street called Raynham Street with only two houses and Robertson's fruit shop. Hilda's friend Pearl and her sister lived up there. 'Oh, they were a very big family...' Her father went down to the shelter where all that was left standing was the door. Inside this doorway was Mr Robertson. 'Dad said, "Come on, let's help you out of there". Dad said he was standing there without a scratch on him. Not a mark. "And I'll help you home". Mr Robertson just collapsed in his arms and died through the blast exploding in his stomach... '.

Hilda's father picked his way through the rubble to the rest of the people. One of Florrie Robertson's sisters had been thrown on her knees, her mother had been blown out and had lost her legs and one of the brothers had lost an eye. 'Dad went towards the mother and she was hunched in what was left of the corner and she said "Oh Mr Waller". He said, "Come on Flo", but she was nearly dead. Then he got hold of her and she died. She was a lovely girl; she had the most lovely ginger hair you ever did see. Oh I was sorry and of course all her family got hurt in that.'

Afterwards they walked further along Old Palace Road. There had been houses from one end to the other on both sides, and then there was not a house left standing. 'The devastation was dreadful, every house went down like a pack of cards and all the rubble went sideways. An old lady I used to look after was buried. She was a little old soul and suffered very dreadful with her chest after being confined for hours.'

That same night Heigham Hall Private Lunatic Asylum was destroyed. 'They were moneyed people who were in Heigham Hall. All we kids could see was this great big building with metal bars coming out of it and people trying to push pillows through the windows. Mr Smalley was the inspector for the gas in the laundry where I was working and at the hall. He said one of the doctors would never let the people go down the air raid shelters, but used to walk them up and down, up and down. Mr Smalley lost his arm up there and one of his legs but we used to feel so sorry for the people because they used to be marching up and down, up and down all night... '.

Another night Hilda did go down the air-raid shelter with several neighbours, the Brown family, Aunt Polly and Hilda's Mother. An incendiary bomb dropped right in the doorway. 'Old Sonny Brown got hold of it and we said, "Don't touch it! Don't touch it!" If that had exploded we would all have got killed inside. He got hold of it and tossed it. That was the closest encounter we ever had.'

Hilda's beloved Donald was away in Italy in the forces. They were supposed to be getting married on 13 June, but Don got his leave postponed for a week and the banns ran out. 'I had to get a special licence. I'd got my dress and I'd got my coat which I'd managed to buy and father had got me a pair of shoes... someone had sent them in [for repair] – lovely blue triple-wedge sandals they were – and never came back for them.'

That was only the half of it. Don and his mother had been bombed out of their house and Hilda's family was persuaded to give him a bed. '"He's got to have a bed, he's been roughing it in the army," she said. So Don was given the front bedroom but was warned, "Don't you go jumping up and down on that bed, the cake is underneath it". In them days you had to feed the springs through the frame, the mattresses weren't like today and sometimes they came off with a twang in the night and I thought of them going through the middle of my cake, but that didn't happen... '. Hilda had put her precious wedding cake under her bed to keep dust off it should there be an air raid! Her mother kept them strictly apart, even on that very morning. Hilda had ironed his trousers – after all she was a trained Hoffman Presser! '"Can I take them upstairs?" I said. "You're not going in his bedroom," she said. "I can't give him his trousers unless I go in the bedroom," I said. When I got there I thought he'd disappeared; he was at the other end of the bed... '. She was afraid he had gone off and left her.

'[Don] said, "Please order the flowers". That was when I worked at Chamberlin's. Well, there was nowhere you could order flowers. So I said to him, "Whatever am I going to do?" They got a couple of roses out of the garden. Mr Pinch had a shop across the street, but the families had no points "because you needed them for foodstuffs...". "Oh,' I said, "We'll have to do without." "No you ain't," he said. "You've been a good girl, you deserve what you get. You look after your Mum and all the family... "'. He gave them a tin of red salmon and a tin of peaches for their wedding breakfast.

Don sold his bike to give the couple the only money they had to get started, seven pounds. They walked to City Hall, Hilda and Don agreeing to meet under the clock. 'I kept looking out for him but of course there are four faces to the clock and he was waiting at the one I wasn't looking at.' Again she thought he'd gone off and left her! 'Anyway, we went in there. We picked up old Nanny, they'd come down from Princes Street and we had our photograph taken at Swains. And then Dad said, "What are we going to do for

The City Hall and Guildhall, where Hilda and Don agreed to

h the clock.

a drink?" I said, "I don't really want one." Don said, "I could do with one", so we walked up to the Haymarket and went in a pub there and he had a half and I had a grapefruit and I ended up with a pain in the stomach all day because of that... We had some salmon and some fruit and a bit of cake, the wedding cake that was still all right. And do you know, in the afternoon we went to the old Regent Cinema on the front row... Don paid for the lot of us out of his seven pounds; he didn't have nothing left by the time he came home... '.

Their first night together was spent in the home of the next-door neighbours. 'I didn't have no place and he didn't have no place... And I tell you, six times that night I had to run out, come out of the bedroom, through the kitchen, out the back door, run across the yard, into the toilet. I never had such pains in my life from that one drink... '.

But Hilda still enjoyed her wedding. Don took most of the cake's top tier back to army camp and later sent a letter back saying, 'The boys enjoyed the wedding cake, will you send me another lump?' So she boxed up the second tier and later the top tier as well. 'So he had all the cake... '. Hilda just wanted something free and easy. 'Not cheap, don't get me wrong. But then again we couldn't afford more 'cos we didn't have the money... I said, "You owe me 17s 6d!" He said, "What for?" I said, "The licence." And I said, "You owe me for the wedding ring." He didn't have any money.'

During another bombing raid, Hilda's father thought Chamberlin's had been hit. '"Oh my God, my daughter works there. I'll have to go down there." "That's down to the floor," they said. "He came down there..."' It was actually Backs and Websters next door. 'They got blown out of that place into the water. It was tragic but you felt for other people, you weren't getting hurt yourself. People were losing people and when they buried them – when we had that massive raid that night, they didn't get an individual grave, they were all buried in one. Well, I don't think they knew who was who to be quite honest...'

As ever, the last word is from Hilda. 'I think that's marvellous to look back and realise what you done and what you learnt because if I hadn't done that I wouldn't know half the things I know now. The way to press clothes and the way to lay things down. 'Cos my mother couldn't teach us nothing [her mother was blind] not how to sew a button on. We had to learn for our own sake.'

Sue Debbage (extracted from audiotape interviews made as part of an oral history study conducted with the Open University in 1999.)

United through war and peace

Mum, Dad, my brother and I lived in Sussex Street in a lovely old two-storey house – or I thought it was lovely. It had quite a large garden with fruit trees, sunken garden with a fishpond and a good-sized lawn. So we had plenty of places to play in. The old house is still there, but it's turned into flats and the garden is now a communal car park.

Dad was a builder and our meal times were always very regular, he'd come home at 12.50 for a 1 o'clock lunch and after he'd eaten, he'd have ten minutes sleep and he'd be back at work again for 1.55. Tea would be at 5.30 prompt, there would be no trays on your laps or grabbing a snack before you went out. Tea was *always* eaten at the table. Each day was very much the same, all planned on a regular basis, even to the Friday night bath and bed with the dreaded spoonful of syrup of figs before you went.

Mum, David and Daphne.

Granny and Grandad.

Granny and Grandad lived next door at No. 29. They both attended the chapel at Wensum Hall, which at that time was in Wensum Street. Granny in particular was always doing something for somebody. She had a simple trust in God and her whole being was committed to those who needed her. She'd bake cakes, sausage rolls and scones for a women's meeting that she'd organise which met every week. Everything that she couldn't cope with she took to God in prayer and left it all to Him.

Often on a Sunday night we'd gather around the piano and sing hymns. I didn't enjoy these evenings very much but I realise now how lucky we were to have such a close family. I often think of the Sunday lunches that we regularly had to eat at Granny's, facing with trepidation the meat on my plate as I was told to 'eat it up' as it was good for me. But I took it home wrapped in my handkerchief. Incidentally, I am now a vegetarian.

Family houses in Sussex Street.

Lunch on Sunday was always prepared on Saturday as it was considered wrong to work on a Sunday. We were not allowed to ride bikes or scooters, just expected to read a book or go for a walk, dressed of course in our Sunday best. It could seem a very long day. Sunday papers were never purchased and granny only went to the cinema once in her whole life and that was to see the Coronation. She was not at all happy about cinemas and saw them as the creation of the devil!

Opposite our house there was a family grocers. A little further up there was a corner shop owned by Mrs Hagen. I know she sold lots of things but the main thing we visited her shop for were toffee apples on a stick, which I think cost a penny. At the corner of Sussex Street and St Augustines was Nicolas the baker, who, for a penny or two, would cook your puddings on his large oven. And on Good Friday, very early in the morning, a baker with a handcart would call 'Hot Cross Buns!' and people would come out of their houses and buy them for their breakfast.

Ice creams were sold from a bicycle with cold containers on the front. Mainly Walls or Eldorado I think. One of the slogans was 'Stop me and buy one.' Every Friday I was given a penny to spend and instructed by my mother not to buy 'any old truck.' I did anyway and had a field day! My friend only had a halfpenny and had to pass her sweets around to the family when she got home. I felt this was most unfair, especially as she had such a large family. As a special treat on a Saturday evening, Dad would take me to Mrs Palmer's for two small packets of Maltesers for David and I, which would be placed under our pillows for the morning. These were called Sunday sweets and probably intended to keep us in bed a bit longer.

Pocket money was usually spent at Mrs Palmer's shop as she had a special counter for children. She also used to make a special ice-cream treat by breaking milk flake into the ice-cream container. I believe her shop was called 'The Dainties'.

St Augustine's at that time was a busy street. I think that at least five public houses and two chemists were in that small area. Mr Cook's chemist traded from the top of the street and Cole's from where the optician is now. Mr Alp the grocer and the fish and chips followed on from there. Hill's pork butcher also traded from the street and I can still smell the sawdust which covered his floor. Mr Pie also had a butcher's shop, just into Pitt Street. When that area was demolished to make way for Anglia Square, his shop stood proud among the weeds and debris until the bitter end and in giant letters across the side of the shop was painted 'we stand alone.'

St Augustine's church where I attended Sunday school still stands, though it is no longer in use. But its immaculate gardens have always been well cared for and still look the same today. The florist was situated immediately after the church. Three worn concrete steps took you into a dark little shop that was owned by a brother and sister. They sold briquettes and firewood as well as flowers and vegetables and even paraffin for oil stoves. Briquettes were a mixture of coal dust and something else, possibly cement dust and they were bonded together to be burned on an open fire to save coal. A barrel organ often stood outside the shop and sometimes my brother would take great delight in turning the handle, much to the annoyance of the organ grinder. Horses and carts were often seen carrying very large loads of all sorts of goods such as coal to various parts of the city. Another 'blast from the past' comes to my mind as I am reminded of being instructed to follow them when they come to our street hoping to obtain manure for my dad's roses. I didn't like this job as I always got the dustbin side of the task while

St Augustine's School.

David pushed the wheelbarrow complete with the contents, if the horses were obliging of course!

I was just eight years old when war broke out. I cannot remember the declaration of war, but expect my parents probably tried to hide it from us as it was all going to be over by Christmas, or so it was said. To say that life changed would be the understatement of the year. At home, a large map of Europe was placed on the wall and map-pins with coloured heads indicated where our soldiers were fighting, while an old radio brought us 'Worker's Playtime,' and 'Force's Favourites.' Every now and again a voice would announce 'this is Lord Haw-haw speaking' and my dad would without fail mutter 'Hello twerp!' Very large posters informed us to 'Dig for Victory,' and that 'Careless talk cost lives.'

At St Augustine's school we had the air-raid drill, hurrying to the shelters instructed by the teachers to walk quietly and not to run. The gas-mask test I hated, as did most children. We had to wear our gas masks and walk through a building, which we imagined was full of gas. But as our gas masks always passed the test, we never did find out what was used. It was really scary, but in those early days of the war, it was mostly due to our vivid imagination.

My best friend Beryl and I shared a desk. She had a tiny pencil sharpener in the shape of Doc of the Seven Dwarves. He was her lucky charm and she always had him in her pocket. One particular afternoon in April 1942, she went home without him. In order that he didn't go astray I took him home with me. That night, some of us from school were scattered in a bombing raid. Beryl and her family were all killed by a direct hit on her house and Norwich was never the same again. Incidentally, that dwarf I always carried with me until about six years ago, when I had my handbag stolen. I guess he was past his sell by date!

That same night I woke up with glass all over my bed, the front windows were hanging out and we were taken into grannies next door. There were two horses tied to a lamppost outside and I was really worried for them. They were terrified but couldn't get away, poor things. We all sat under grannies heavy dining table. David and I with our hands over our ears still unable to shut out the crump of bombs falling. It was strange to see the city so bright with the light of fires started by the incendiary bombs, especially as we had been used to blackouts for such a long while. In the morning, the extent of the damage was revealed, including the loss of the city railway station, which was completely destroyed. The station was very close to us.

Later on in the war, we shared an Anderson shelter with neighbours, Mrs Elliot and her family from No. 31. It always seemed damp and cold, but we didn't care. It was a safe feeling in there. And they were company for mum as dad was a fireman and always called out during the air raids. Later on at the Blyth school, when we were in an air-raid shelter, everyone sang, probably to shut out the noise. But I remember a girl with a wonderful voice, I think her name was Sheila, being repeatedly asked to sing 'Vienna city of my dreams' and whenever I hear that song I think of the air-raid shelters.

Leaving the Blyth school at fifteen against my parent's wishes, meant I had to find a job and the five pounds fine for leaving school early had to be paid by me. I went to work for Freeman, Hardy & Willis and was paid the

National Fire Service, Bethel Street, 1940. Daphne's dad is first left at the front of the crew.

A family outing with Daphne's mum and dad on the far right, c. 1926,

vast sum of 22s 6d per week. I had to pay 15s board money, 5s towards the fine and 2s 6d for coffee money. Grateful as I was for the job I only stayed about six months, but I never walk past that mosaic tile entrance to that shop without remembering how I had to scrub it on my hands and knees and clean all the brasses every morning. I was very relieved before long to start my intended career as a Post Office telephonist, but that is another story.

Daphne Dennis
(Transcribed from an audiotaped interview)

Not all doom and gloom

It was 22 December 1928 when I was brought into this world. Born at Seven Star Norwich, I was to be one of eleven children. I was named Valerie Anne by my mother and father, Elizabeth Mary and Leonard. I spent the following years growing up in and around Norwich and must have quite liked the place because I've lived here all my life.

Norwich has inevitably changed over the years, people have come and gone, factories have been demolished and new places have been built. However, I'm sure those who are old enough to remember will frequently reminisce about the way things used to be.

I was a child during the war. My first memory of it was when it all began in 1939. I was ten years old and I can remember being at home and hearing lots of shouting from outside. My father, who was in bed, called to us 'Get dressed! Get dressed!' and, quick as a flash, he was up, out and gone.

Thorpe St Andrew.

The people shouting outside had seen the newspapers announcing the start of the Second World War. My father had previously served in the army, so he was called as a reserve. That's why he'd rushed out of the house so quickly. Back in those days, in the same way as today, my father as a reserve would be one of the first to go to war. And he did. But he was one of the lucky ones who returned. Many didn't.

Obviously being a child during the war, I was not aware of how the war would affect the rest of the world. But I was aware of how the war changed our lives completely. We stopped living normal lives. We started doing strange things, like sleeping under the stairs. I can remember being there at night with my brothers and sisters. As we lay there, I could feel the floor shake every time our guns were fired, but after a while this strange behaviour became part of our new routines. Every part of our lives changed, whether we were at home, at work or at school. There was no running away from the war.

My first school was Thorpe Hamlet School. Every pupil was quick to learn the rules. No 'buts' or 'maybes,' if there was an attack we had to hide under our desks as quick as we could, or if we were in the playground we had to lay down flat on the floor. There were fun times too, though. It wasn't all doom and gloom, at least not if you were a child growing up in wartime. Where the Heartsease Estate now stands, there were once fields. In fact there used to be an airfield. A German plane came down in those fields once. I'm not certain if it was shot down or if it simply crashed, but I can remember lots of children scrambling about the wreckage, looking for souvenirs to take home. Its funny, nowadays, apart from being considered highly dangerous, I doubt many children would even be interested in taking home pieces of a crashed plane!

Remembering back to school times again, one morning we were walking to school as usual but when we got there, well... it wasn't! Our school had been bombed. Fortunately it had happened at night so no one was hurt, but that meant we had to attend a new school. From then on we mingled in with the already present pupils at Stewart School in Telegraph Lane. You can imagine how daunting it was for little me, aged eleven, after all, Stewart School was a senior school. But after a while, we all fitted in just fine. Even though it was a new school the drills were just the same. As soon as we heard the air raid sirens we all had to head for the shelters. One day it felt like we'd been underground for hours and hours. In fact we had spent the entire morning in the shelter. One by one, mothers collected each child until I was the last child left. My teacher and I waited patiently but came to the conclusion that my mother wasn't coming to get me. Well, she did have my brothers and sisters to look after. So my teacher said she would take me home in her car. I was secretly quite pleased my mother hadn't arrived because I'd never been in a motorcar before. Then, just as we were about to leave, along comes mother. As you've probably guessed, I was a little upset to say the least and ended up throwing a bit of a tantrum. It was only years later when I became a mother and when I look back at times like this, that I realise how awful it must've been bringing up a family in such as difficult time, fearing for their lives and their safety. Sorry mother!

Stewart school was my last place of education. I left school the day I turned fourteen which was 22 December 1942 and I started work on the 27 (the day after Boxing Day) we didn't hang about. My mother took me to get my job because I was too shy to go in on my own.

I began working at Harmer's where my sister, Audrey, was already employed. Harmer's was a factory that made clothes and soldier's uniforms. It had several premises dotted about in Norwich. One particularly chilly morning I can remember getting up and going downstairs for breakfast. Father, who was at home that morning, had made a lovely fire to keep us all warm and a big pile of toast too. We were all about to tuck in when my father announced, 'No need to hurry with your breakfast today girls! Harmer's isn't there any more, it got firebombed last night.' It took a fortnight for Harmer's to find new premises, so we got a small break. Oh how places change. If you'd recently taken a trip to see where our factory site once was, you'd have found St Andrew's car park. Today even that is being demolished. I wonder what will be built there next?

The war destroyed many lives and many places. Where Debenhams is now, I can remember huge craters in the ground where bombs landed. Over the years, these old scars have been covered up. Unfortunately human scars, especially mental ones, are a little trickier to heal. We all have different stories we remember about the war, some good, some bad. But the one thing that it taught us all was to appreciate life, because in just one second it can be taken away. I can still remember clearly the day it was announced that the war was over. A victory for England – hurrah! A day that will be remembered for all of time. People held street parties to celebrate the homecoming and photographers took pictures so they could sell you a copy to keep. I had my picture taken with

Victory Party, 1945.

lots of others. It represented a new start. We could live our lives without fear. We were the children of the future.

A couple of years later another part of my life was to begin. I met a wonderful man called Bertie and on 27 November 1947 I became his wife. We were married at the registry office, City Hall – one of the few buildings that are still around today. I like to think that our wedding was just that extra bit special. The reason being we got married exactly one week after the Queen got married. On Thursday, like the Queen, and at 11 o'clock just like the Queen. Bertie wore a navy blue pin-striped suit and I wore a powder blue suit with a pink carnation. I might not have looked exactly like the queen but I certainly did feel like royalty.

As time went by, I went on to have four lovely children and over the years I've become a grandmother. In fact I've recently become a very proud great-grandmother. Unfortunately Bertie is no longer with us but I am sure he would have made a wonderful great-grandfather.

By the way, just in case you're wondering, I did eventually get my ride in a motor car. These days most families own a car but as we all know lots of material things that were once considered a luxury are now taken for granted. Although people's everyday lives have changed in many ways since 1945, it would be nice to think that one thing still remains: the ability to appreciate what we have and accept the things we don't. For the most important thing in life is to treasure our loved ones, our family and friends and our memories of those who cannot be with us today.

Valerie Harley

Valerie and Bertie's wedding day 27 November 1947.

Wartime Christmas happiness

How well I remember the excitement of those Christmas parties! So that my mother could be involved in war work to supplement the family's finances, I began school at the age of four. Thus, these Christmas memories are a mix of the three Christmases of the American 'invasion' of our Norfolk village.

All remembrances tell us that summers were hot and winters were cold, but those winters really were cold! Bone cold! Ice inside the windowpanes cold! Baths before the fire cold! So when Christmas approached and the adult's faces were gloomy and glum from the news of the war, we children were entranced when, one dark November afternoon the infant schoolroom door burst open, shattering the enforced silence. Our diminutive headmistress, dressed in her uniform tailored suit, brought us a visitor who seemed so tall that our heads were tilted back to view the blonde giant of a man, twisting the peak of his cap between fidgety fingers.

Forty pairs of eyes followed their progress across the boarded floor to our teacher's desk. Already on her feet she raised her palms upwards. With a scraping of chairs we chorused our 'Good Afternoon' and then strained our well-trained ears to pick up the threads of their conversation, which I repeated a few hours later at the supper table. 'And they're coming to collect us and take us to a lovely party at the Base.' (The Base had become central to the lives of so many people from the surrounding villages.)

We children had no knowledge of the goings on at the Base: it was, to us, a place where the droning aeroplanes woke us up as they took off each morning. A place we cycled to on a Sunday afternoon to see the great B24s skimming the hedgerows and a place where, to us, hundreds and thousands of virile young gods lived and worked. We admired these gods who sailed along on their bikes at high speeds, throwing candy to the children as they went. We boasted to each other about how many of these gods we knew, how many we counted sitting on the five-barred gates chewing on grass stems and waving, 'Hi, kids!'

What a deliciously incorrect way of speaking, we thought, as we practised it while languidly dawdling to the village school. We also knew that most of these smartly dressed gods were treated with suspicion by the mothers of young women. Later, of course, we all discovered that they had just cause, as the birth-rate rose and tongues clicked and then silenced in our presence. Those gods had feet of clay! But to us children muffled and mittened in the 4 o'clock twilight of the long-awaited December day, the day of the party had come at last!

A cold wind ruffled the canvas sides of the huge USAF lorries. We shivered in our excitement and, as discipline extended beyond the classroom, our three teachers 'tut tutted' as we were lifted aloft, giggling, by strong arms. 'Hey! Bobby, there's a black boy going to drive us!' stage-whispered ten-year-old David. 'Sure thing, man!' We all jumped, startled, as the large young Negro turned to peer through the flaps. I vividly remember thinking that I'd never seen so many white teeth or such white whites to someone's eyes. From four to fourteen years old we were mixed and mismatched in those lorries which drew away from the school and trundled their cargo bumpily through the narrow country lane. I can only liken my first impression of our arrival at the cavernous hangar to the ending of the 1980s film ET.

Wartime restrictions meant blackout during the hours of darkness, but for one brief marvellous moment when the backflaps of the canvas were raised we all sucked in our breaths. We exhaled an 'ooh' and 'ahh.' Lights of all colours laced like shining necklaces across the hangar, multi-coloured streamers criss-crossed the dizzy height and baubles and bells glistened and glowed gloriously! And over there, at the end, on a dais, stood the statuesque statement of Christmas itself: an enormously high fir tree, topped with a five-fingered star, all aglow, with real candles on alternate branches. Altogether, we were ushered in by these brash but kindly men who had delivered their last consignment of children – for three other villages' school children were there – their mouths also open, gazing at the workmanship of their benefactors.

'Well, kids – welcome!' the station commander was saying.

All heads turned to him. 'You look slightly bewildered! Now take off your coats and hats because you're going to have a real good time! We hope that you're going to enjoy the tea our cooks have laid on for you and we sure wish you all have a pleasant stay with us!' For a few seconds there was silence and then someone began clapping and we all clapped and clapped for the sheer pleasure of thanking them for what lay ahead of us in that magical place – so far from the restrictions of war.

It was utter, utter, bliss! I had never seen so much food as at that party; strange food like Frankfurter sausages, fine food like the mountains of salmon sandwiches and exotic food like tinned fruit and ice cream! Ice cream I had no memories of, but I well recall being told that day, 'Come along little lady, have some more, it may be a little while before you have it again.' It certainly wasn't until after the war that my mother tried to bring one from Norwich – six miles away by bus!

Of course Charley Bennington boasted: 'We used to have ice cream three times a day before old Hitler took it all!' We all had to believe him, as we had no proof of the alternative. Naturally Rosie and her little brother were sick through over-eating and of course every school has to have some of its members letting the side down by causing a puddle, but that meal was memorable in every way. Carols and songs were played over loud speakers for us and, as we slowly thawed out, our enjoyment grew. We chattered and giggled and clapped our pleasure through the showing of cartoon films and threw ourselves gaily into a series of well organised party games until the arrival of Father Christmas, or Santa Claus as our American hosts called him.

We were all loudly dancing the conga, coiled around the hangar when we first saw him and, as the music gently faded, we approached him to receive our Christmas

'Wartime Christmas' from an illustration by Mrs V. Turner.

present. We were then guided to the bran-tub to dig deeply to bring up a cellophane bag of candy. Joy of all joys – sweets!

As those lorries carried us back to the school and our waiting mothers, we lustily sang along with Chuck and Hank and Bill and Daryl 'Mares eat oats and does it eats and little lambs eats ivy!' A silly song to end a fantastic party, given each year by those big, kind, warm-hearted men called Yanks.

Valerie Turner

4 Local Legends

Late Victorian matriarchs

Among those with a tenuous hold on the social rockface in the 1930s was Polly Culyer, spinster, in the parish of St Paul, Norwich. Miss Culyer is described in Kelly's 1933 Directory of Norwich as a dressmaker, to be found at No. 5 St Paul's Square, although she had been retired for several years when, as a child, I knew her through my play in the narrow alley behind our tiny terraced houses.

St Paul's Square in those days was a leafy enclave, circling a tiny medieval church, in an ancient quarter of the city. The Square had been described towards the end of the nineteenth century as 'red-brick cottages having replaced a rookery of disgraceful tenements, under the Artisans' Dwelling Act.' It was still peopled by poor families, but for whom the description 'respectable' was important.

Giant plane trees in the churchyard overreached the pavements, giving shade on

St Paul's Square today.

hot summer evenings, which were often sweetened by the passing of the horse-drawn water cart, as its jets lay the dust. On these occasions residents could often be found sitting outside their front doors, chatting and generally reinforcing their sense of community. At the same time there pervaded a realisation that each family's hold on what was paradise, compared with the bug-ridden slums which proliferated nearby, was ever imperilled by the vicissitudes of the shoe industry, to which all working males and most of the single females were in thrall. Unspoken also was the common fear of the proximity of poverty and the final step down – the workhouse.

Polly was a sweet elderly lady on whose deeply-lined face years of hardship had been engraved, although when she smiled one could feel the warmth. This dressmaker had never made more than a precarious living but had become expert at surviving on that narrow margin of genteel poverty which lay between comfort and the ultimate degradation that the workhouse represented.

In an almost mystical way Polly gave the impression of, in old age, having serenely transcended all earthly difficulties and was confidently looking forward to her heavenly reward. In this respect she well-personified the Victorian shibboleth that those who suffer most in this life will enjoy greater blessings in the next – a philosophy which those in very comfortable circumstances also seemed strangely able to support.

However, it was my habit to offer daily to the residents of the Square a shopping service, by custom being rewarded with a halfpenny for each errand successfully accomplished – a facility of which Miss Culyer took advantage. She would call me into her tiny back parlour to discuss her requirements, front rooms were used only for funerals, weddings and the major Christian festivals, and to ensure I memorised her needs. The room itself was furnished in early Victorian style, with heavy damask curtains keeping out much of the light. The same material formed the tablecloth and its dark green colour glowed goldly also in the pelmet which hung from the mantle shelf. On entering the room from the sunny back yard it took several seconds for one's eyes to adjust to the gloom.

Polly herself was usually dressed – furnished might be a better word – in several layers of different materials, in one shade of brown or another. These would be topped with a mobcap, effectively obviating any accurate assessment of her age and whatever shape she had taken up by this time: the whole ensemble depicting a time capsule of an earlier age.

That was, of course, an age of great eccentrics but Polly also had her own diversion from the houseproud habits of the other local ladies. She never dusted. One effect being that when I placed her purchases on the table a tiny cloud of dust would kick up and its subtle, distinctive but not unpleasant odour remains in memory with me still. On mature reflection I think of Miss Culyer as a rather more cheerful version of Dicken's Miss Haversham.

Other scents sometimes mysteriously return. The metallic smell of the zinc bath in which I was placed every evening before the weekly dose of syrup of figs was forced down my throat. My parent's clothing heavily impregnated with the redolence of the leather in which their working lives were submerged. The different tobacco fragrances emanating from the various brands of cigarette cards I begged from the men leaving-off from the local factory. In summer, the strong smell of tar as the heat melted the surface of the wooden blocks that formed the surface of many of the city streets. Most pungent of all, the mouth-watering promise made by the bloaters

St Paul's Square today.

grilled over my grandmother's living-room fire.

Grandmother was one of the other Victorians who lived in the Square. Christened Mariah, but known as Riah, she and her sister Alice made a formidable pair, and with Polly in tow, at the outbreak of war they became known as the ARP.

Grandmother was most impressive. Five feet tall, she took size one shoes and was proud of her tightly corseted eighteen-inch waist. But she had a presence that paradoxically dwarfed everyone else. Often frustrated in argument, my grandfather would tower over his wife and demand to know, 'Who is the master here?' – to which she would calmly reply, with a basilisk smile, 'You of course are the master Albert – but I am the mistress.' He would stump off, gnashing his teeth and muttering about 'alterations here.' But we all knew that his effective authority would never extend much beyond the walls of his tiny shed, which had been grafted on to the back of the house.

I never knew boredom in the square, leaving at seven years of age, and even on my last day making faces at Mrs Barnes' pet monkey, which lived indoors, normally perched on the windowsill and which could be reliably driven to distraction in this way.

I recall with affection Miss Polly Culyer, dressmaker, of St Paul's Square and the many others I closely observed at that stage of my life. I admire the fortitude and strength of character they demonstrated in the face of the poverty, insecurity and disease which was never far away and as a result of which the frequent casualties in their midst served to remind them not to ask for whom the bell tolled.

John Ferguson

The reign of 'Black Anna'
Prize-winning entry

'If you like me, like me – if you don't, I won't twist your arm.' Those were the words of 'Black Anna,' a proud and principled woman whose warmth of character charmed all who met her. She was known as the 'singing landlady' of the Jolly Butchers in Ber Street. It was a partnership that was to last for over four decades. Renowned for her jazz singing and her no nonsense approach, she made the Jolly Butchers the most famous pub in Norwich.

Born Antoinette Carrara in 1905 of Italian parents; Anna lived in Norwich all her life. Her liking for dressing in black was one reason she became known as 'Black Anna,' 'I haven't worn colours since I was a girl,' she used to tell her customers. Anne, or Anna as she was known, inherited both her mother's looks and fine singing voice. With her jet black hair piled high on her head, swinging earrings and long flowing dresses, Anna had her own distinctive style. Her appearance gave her the sobriety of an Italian matron, which was as much a part of the scene as the pub itself. But although her continental looks and Italian warmth of expression was not belied by her ancestry, her accent certainly was, for it was broad Norfolk.

In 1935 Anna and her husband took over the Jolly Butchers as Mr and Mrs Jack Hannent. They had one daughter. The pub was situated in one of the oldest streets in Norwich and was central to Anna's roots. It was in and around Ber Street that the Italian colony, who migrated to Norwich around 1880, settled. Jack and Anna jointly ran the Jolly Butchers for the next few years making it home for themselves and their daughter, Jacqueline. When Jack decided to leave, Anna applied to continue the tenancy. Anna took over the pub and lodging house – for the Jolly Butchers had the reputation of being the last common lodging house in Norwich.

It became home to labourers, tradesmen and musicians, who got cheap accommodation provided they were prepared to muck in at the pub. The focal point of the house was the large downstairs kitchen with its tiled floor and iron cooking range. This was kept alight day and night and was where the lodgers prepared their meals. It was in this communal area that Anna enjoyed their company and her many roles overlapped – pub landlady, jazz singer, confidante, counsellor and friend. With an ability and stamina that was unparalleled, Anna was as tough as Ber Street itself.

It was Anna's love of singing for which most people will remember her. As a girl she sang the Italian operatic airs she learnt from her mother, Lizabetta. But it was not until the war that jazz got a hold of her.

During the war German bombs destroyed much of Ber Street, but the Georgian pub survived. It was around 1942 that the American serviceman discovered the small pub and Anna took to jazz singing saying, 'I found the Americans liked that type of singing so I went in for it: it was good for trade.' It was from the Americans that Anna learnt most of her songs and was singing 'Silver Dollar' and 'Watermelon Baby' long before they gained popularity over here. When the US airmen discovered her they found that she had a voice that was quite unlike a woman's. She often recalled an incident when an American Lieutenant walked into the public bar and asked, 'Who is the man singing in the other room?' With her deep husky voice Anna developed a style of an artist who could sing American music with a spirit and gusto that was quite un-English. This endeared her to the American customers, many of who became regulars through the war years and kept in touch when they returned home. Anna's love of jazz was drawn towards blues, which suited her deep and powerful tones. Her idol was the legendary Sophie Tucker. It was through blues singing, although she also continued with jazz, calypso and a touch of gospel, that Anna built up a devoted following. It was the Americans who dubbed her the 'English Sophie Tucker,' with the Sophie Tucker touch and the Sophie Tucker figure; Anna was sixteen stone and made no secret of it.

'Black Anna' had the vigour of a performer who lived her music. It was a way of life for her and when asked about her singing she would say, 'You don't sing jazz, you feel it, it is something inside you that you are telling. Maybe you don't realise it, but the audience does.' Many will have vivid memories not only of the Jolly Butchers and Anna's singing but also of the jovial atmosphere. For Anna liked to laugh – hands on hips, head back, delivering a gutsy laugh that set her double chin quivering unashamedly and rocking her large frame to its very core.

Anna's popularity remained throughout the 1950s, '60s and '70s as an extraordinary woman with a powerful voice whose reputation became known countrywide. Customers of all ages flocked to the little pub in Ber Street to hear her. She also achieved success on the stage and at jazz festivals singing with

'Black Anna' in 1967. (courtesy Eastern Daily Press*)*

Acker Bilk, George Melly, Chris Barber and Terry Lightfoot. Anna could easily have turned professional but her heart remained with her pub and the people who patronised it. She used to say, 'I never wanted to turn professional because it is just a rat race. If I am in the mood, I will sing to a thousand people for nothing because I love it'. Professional or not Anna attracted celebrities to her premises for the quality of her performance and her style. When Danny La Rue was filming in the city he gave a party for her. She had friends all over the world. She had no affections.

Anna's audiences were good humoured and cheery. It was the unique atmosphere and great music that 'Black Anna' brought to the pub with her love of jazz that earned her the title 'the queen of jazz.' For when the woman in black stepped out from behind the bar to sing, one look called the pub to order and everybody listened. Standing on her box, as Anna invariably did, she sang old time jazz with some songs near the knuckle but always with the chorus line for the crowd to sing along with. Informality and audience participation were a part of her performance, 'I might fool around sometimes – go cross-eyed or pull a funny face,' she'd say, but it worked and she became one of the city's best loved characters. From the '60s, on Tuesdays, Anna had what she called her 'club night,' but there was no club, although the door of the music room was kept firmly shut and only customers known to like a 'cooler' brand of jazz and blues were admitted.

Anna sang somewhat less during the last two years of her life but could always be relied on to belt out a few old favourites. From the '70s she was usually supported by John Ayres on piano, Mike Winton on drums, Mike Parle on banjo Andrew Bowie on clarinet and Robert Hodgson on guitar. Throughout her life Anna fiercely guarded her privacy and that of her lodgers. She may have spoken the Mediterranean language of open flowing gestures and movement with her hands but her lips remained firmly sealed. Towards the end of her life if anyone had the cheek to ask her age she would fix them with her dark flashing eyes and reply, 'just turned sixty.'

Anna reigned for forty-one years. She died peacefully in May 1976, following a brief spell of ill health. During this time her daughter, Jacqueline, managed the business and entertained the customers in the irrepressible style of her mother.

A month after Anna's death a packed house gathered at the Jolly Butchers to honour the very jolly Mrs Antoinette Hannent. That night she was remembered along with the glory days of her and her pub in a tribute that got the joint jumping. As queen of the Norwich night scene she would have been delighted. Anna loved it when people joined in the singing and used to say, 'I love crowds: I play on an audience and find an audience likes to be part of the act. When they start singing with me, I know I have got them.' To the people of Norwich, 'Black Anna' *was* the Jolly Butchers. Her singing and principled approach gained her celebrity style status. Whether she was comfortable with this is hard to say, for she courted people not fame. But one thing is certain our memories of her and her immense personality will never fade. We loved you 'Black Anna'. We loved you a lot.

Since Anna's death the Jolly Butchers has re-opened briefly as a public house in the 1980s. It then stood empty for a number of years before being sold and used as offices. It was most recently purchased in 1999 by a charitable trust and is presently being used to help families in need.

Jenny Fox

'Play that ol' piana'

Listening to music and reading still fill a large part of our leisure hours, although today the vast proportion of such entertainment is pre-packaged and served up by electronic means. In the immediate post war era reading was limited, for books were scarce and paper at a premium. Access to 'ready made' music was by the 'wireless', or the gramophone, other than that one had to furnish one's own entertainment; it was here that the 'pianoforte' reigned supreme. Every respectable drawing room or public bar was incomplete without the 'piana'! Returning servicemen from the 1939 war would spend their 'gratuity' on the instrument with the hope that one of the family would 'larn t' play'; some did this better than others! Indentured to a piano firm, I was thrust into this post-war boom, charged with the task of returning 'blitzed' and otherwise damaged instruments into circulation.

In the heart of Norwich a cellar was filled with the survivors of the 'blitzkrieg' awaiting the surgery that would make them presentable to a waiting public. 'Presentable' was quite a tall order; panels were often full of broken glass and the wooden 'actions' full of plaster or other debris from bombed buildings, but time never seemed to matter as it does today. With simple materials and hours of patient effort, former complete wrecks were wheeled over the road to take their place in the showroom. Once in the window, there they stood, proudly glowing in their new coat of 'French polish' admired by all.

The armed forces 'concert party spirit' which has served so well in wartime was carried through the 1950s, by which time I had already been dispatched into an unsuspecting world as a 'tuner'. Village halls, public houses, church halls were my daily bread and for my cake I might be honoured by a commission to tune at a great concert hall in preparation for the arrival of a famous name in music – 'Solomon' comes to mind. The lot of the travelling pianoforte tuner, rather like that of the policeman in the *Pirates of Penzance*, was not always a happy one, for exposed to all weathers and without the ubiquitous petrol motorcar, cycling

'Tuning in the church' from an illustration by Anthony Ward.

remained the principal transport for Norwich. Beyond the city boundary, one relied on omnibus and the railway.

Omnibus was all very well for a compact round in a small market town, but once in the market square, with a heavy bag of tools, coils of spare steel strings and other necessary impedimenta, one felt very much alone wandering unfamiliar streets. The brighter side of this alien environment came from the countrywomen, who always took pity on this strange young man. He was the 'visitor from the big city' and their contact with the outside world. To be a 'housewife' in the middle of the last century was a declaration of pride, as opposed to today when not to

have a 'chosen career' is regarded as an admission of failure. Then, to be a farmer's wife, or the teamsman's wife, made you queen of your domain. Should the 'queen' be the musical one of the family woe betide the sloppy itinerant who did not 'temper his fifths evenly', or left a 'wave' on his unisons.

Working alone with strong-minded and attractive women was not without its disadvantages, for one did tend to get bullied! The ability to absorb large quantities of tea and many slices of Victoria sandwich was as important as the job in hand. Once satisfied that all was correct, a well-known popular test piece had to be played. Arthur Wood's 'Barrick Green' ('The Archers') always went down well in the farmhouse. 'Rustle of Spring' made a good encore; but one had to beware of the enthusiastic music lover who would propose a duet. The waltz 'Destiny' was easily divided into four hands. More dangerous was to agree to a four handed Polonaise by Chopin. This meant sitting very close to a warm and commanding farmer's wife full of philharmonic ecstasy, only to be surprised by an authoritative farmer who was not very sure as to where all this was leading. Oh yes! It did happen! And it was possible to be too 'gallant' in the country.

One day a 'Boudoir Grand' had to be moved but the 'gentlemanly gentleman' insisted that it was unwise for the daughter of the house to assist, as the instrument 'was extremely heavy'. The gentleman was told in no uncertain fashion that: 'I can carry a two-coombe sack of barley as good as any man!' We moved it as a pair. Shades of feminism to come? The cynic might ask at this point 'How is it that this young man is constantly surrounded by delightful women'? No! I am not 'shooting a line'! At the time, in country districts, the men worked outside whilst the women would stay at home, to look after the house and the children. Whether this was good or bad is not for me to say but that is why and how this situation arose.

A more flexible form of transport was to take the bicycle on a train. Norwich had two passenger stations: Thorpe Norwich and Norwich City, both in the care of British Railways. Norwich City still retained much of its 'Muddle and Go Nowhere' atmosphere inherited from when the Midland Railway joined forces with the speedy Great Northern Railway in order to break the monopoly of the hard worked Great Eastern. As a result of this 1870 collaboration, a single line wandered from Norwich vaguely north-west, with the hope that it would eventually connect with South Lynn and the Western World.

Association with the M & GN was through an experimental advertisement in the *Norfolk News*, which brought contact with (to me) an unknown RAF outpost near Raynham Park. Here a group of service wives were arranging a recital by a not very well known pianist. Most communication in those days was by letter; indeed, it was over a year before I had a telephone installed in the workshop. After much exchanging of letters, enough venues were set up to make it worth my while to adventure to the far west. It sounds impossible now but in those days the forty miles between Melton Constable in the centre of Norfolk and the port of King's Lynn seemed little different to travelling from say, King's Lynn to Montreal in Canada. So, stowing my trusted bicycle on the train, I ventured forth into the unknown.

I had never given much thought to international friends or enemies, Russians were big chaps who sang great chorus songs like 'It's a longer longer vay toos Tipperary!' Americans were perhaps nearer my line as they included chaps like Scott Joplin who composed catchy 'rags' – piano pieces of considerable merit like 'Black and White Rag' (Remember Pot Black!). After a few false starts I found myself in a guardroom with a very suspicious RAF policeman who convinced me that Norfolk was flooded with spies aiming 'to overthrow democracy'. Needless to say I was rescued by forceful ladies who were much more concerned about my well being than the end of democracy. When they found that I was the piano tuner and not the pianist this welcome was slightly muted but I was well cared for, even to the extent that a truck was commandeered to take my bicycle and me to the next venue. It was a big round and darkness had fallen before I reached the level crossing gates of Hillington, more by accident than by design. After a short wait on the platform a 'Wells Fargo' locomotive arrived with three carriages and a guards van. The kindly guard secured my bicycle to the rails on the side of the van, then offered me the seat in his side vestibule, so I could 'see the signals', with the added warning of: 'Don't let no-one see you or you'll git me the sack!' What a gentleman!

Trips on the Midland and Great Northern were few and far between; but it was a delightful way of travelling provided that time was no object. The timetable *was* kept to, trains *did* arrive on time and although the carriages were often shabby the station staff were an item of politeness. In contrast to the M & GN the former London and North Eastern still retained a jumble of lines and branches covering Norfolk from the coast inland to Wymondham Junction, a few miles west of Norwich. From this tiny railway paradise it was possible to take the 'Crab and Winkle' branch northward to the coastal resort of Wells on Sea.

With the ancient Saxon Cathedral as a centre (Station: LNER North Elmham) a 'round' was established extending some twenty miles along the railway line to finish at Wells on Sea. Any further north and they would have needed to send the Wells' life-boat out to fetch me back! Seeing that pianos need attention about twice a year this strange young man, with the dark suit, Anthony Eden hat, starched collar and the incongruous pedal cycle, became a familiar sight, a sort of 'railway pet', on the 'Crab and Winkle'. The familiar face of the guard beamed from the gloom of his van as another adventure began. 'Going north?' he would enquire, before stowing the bicycle by the door ready to be dropped off at Wymondham junction. Here one waited until eventually a tiny 'Queen Mary' locomotive chuffed out of the miniature 'loco' (depot) bringing with it two coaches, or on a really good day, three! The new guard would smile as he took the bicycle and warn me if any of the Queen Mary's soot had marked my starched white collar before I retreated to the compartment and the journey to the far north began.

The strategy was to travel by rail to the furthest point from Norwich then work back, for it was not always possible to finish a 'round' to coincide with the departure time of the homeward bound train. In dire circumstances one could reach the main line by bicycle, this giving a better chance of boarding any suitable train, rather than being marooned at the far end of a little used branch line. If the wooden 'action' had to be brought back to the workshop, the weather was dry and not too windy the 'action' was extracted from the case, then walked back to the station, supported on the pedal of the bicycle. This was not as horrendous as it might sound, because, then, road traffic was minimal and there was always a friendly porter waiting outside the station to carry the unwieldy object to the guard's van. It was also a marvellous sign of trust when the customer allowed this precious and fragile object to be wheeled away on a wobbling bicycle.

Occasionally thoughtless customers caused agony, such as when I was called out to an ailing piano that I had not seen before, shortly to become the centre of an important social festival. Here always, a sort of 'law of inverse proportions' prevailed, in that: the worse the condition of the piano, the more urgent the need time-wise. Further constraint came when the owner claimed great attachment to what was really a worn out liability. Trying to tell the local gamekeeper, who was renowned for his short temper, that his great-grandfather's treasure was a worm-eaten heap of rubbish, was even more dangerous than being found practising duets with his attractive wife!

Was I propositioned from time to time? The short answer is yes! But the era was not conducive to 'loose living' and certainly nothing like the steamy scenes we see on our modern television screens. Public houses brought contact with all sorts, including those women who simply wanted money, although these ladies were not without their good points. I remember a large and very drunken gentleman who became so annoyed with the regular 'ping' of the hammer striking a particularly unresponsive string deciding that he would smash the 'fall' (key cover) down on my fingers, thus putting me out of business for good. Two ladies of the street thwarted his desire and saved me from severe injury, 'He's a good lad you leave him alone!' they chorused, the man fled and I am still able to write this today!

In small market towns frequent visits associated the tuner with *the family* who organised the 'culture' of the district: the choir, the drama group and the Gilbert and Sullivan Society. In these welcoming surroundings there was a tendency to let one's guard down and become complacent. All would be well unless one day that the lady of the house greeted you alone with tales of how dull life was out in the Norfolk wilderness. This was the time to put your tuning hammer back in the bag and insist that you meet your train. There are many reasons for loving railways but this particular one is rarely quoted. No! I never succumbed! But I was sorely tempted. Norfolk breeds some delightful ladies who tend to become more attractive as the years pass rather than less. But now, like Father William, I have become old, the steam locomotives have gone, the parlour piano has gone: even that satisfaction of seeing a job well done is in decline.

But those memories of Chaminade's 'Autumn' played four hands, and the cheery porter holding the level crossing gate as the bicycle was pushed up the ramp to the platform... Then for good measure there was the kindly locomotive driver and fireman who lured me onto their footplate. Not so much as an eyelid was lifted until I was about to leave my last call, where the lady of the house suggested I might benefit by a visit to the bathroom. Well! I was filthy! My normally snow-white collar was black with coal dust, my face striped grey below where my forehead met my hatband. 'Had a good day?' asked the stationmaster. 'Better ride in here; I'll look after y' bike!' The smile as he held that carriage door for me was positively evil; I wonder where he is now?

Anthony Ward

Nurse Edith Cavell

The photograph shows the grave of Nurse Edith Cavell, patriot and martyr. She was a nurse in occupied Belgium during the First World War, though as well as nursing she was helping allies caught behind the lines escape back to Britain. The Germans discovered this and on 12 October 1915 executed her. In 1919 her remains were returned to the UK and she was reburied in Norwich Cathedral at the request of her family who came from Swardeston, just outside Norwich. There is a more permanent memorial to Nurse Cavell in Tombland.

Sarah Skinner

Edith Cavell's grave, post-1919.

5 My Norwich – A Fine City

Colegate - the street of light

Norwich has many interesting highways and byways. Everyone knows Elm Hill, while the beautiful Cathedral Close is like a village at the heart of the city. But, for me, one street leaves them all standing – not only in the variety of its buildings and the richness of its history, but in the lessons it teaches about the character of its citizens. I've lived there for thirty years. It's the best street in the city!

Colegate dates back over 1,200 years, to days when Norwich was a collection of Saxon and Danish settlements, still to coalesce. It lies in the centre of the city, north of the River Wensum, in the area known for centuries as Over-the-Water. From the Saxon settlement of Coslany, this

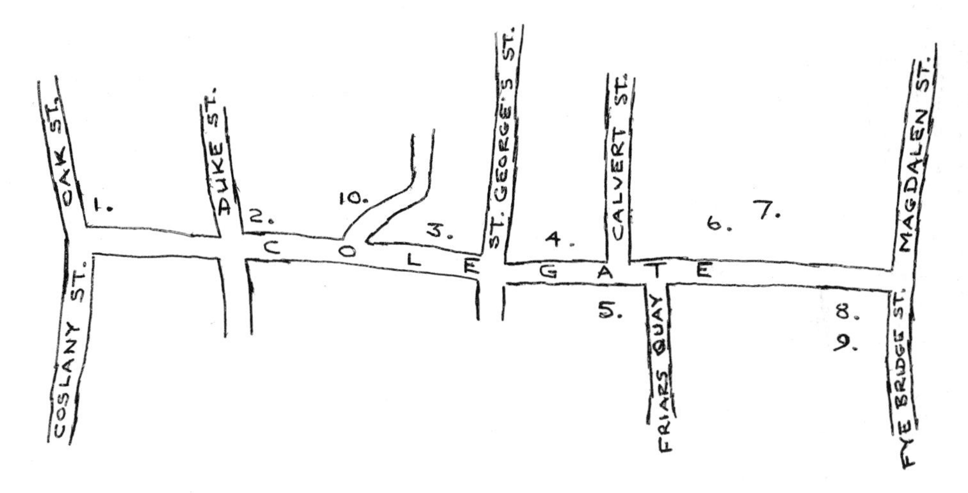

Key:
1. St Miles
2. The Golden Star
3. St George, Colegate
4. Bacon's House
5. The Merchants of Colegate
6. The Octagon chapel
7. The Old Meeting House
8. St Clement at Fye Bridge
9. The Mischief Tavern
10. The Woolpack

Above: *Map of Colegate, drawn by Jack Burton.*

Opposite: *Aerial view of Norwich, pre-1960.*

A view of Colegate in quieter times taken by Jack Burton.

marshy, riverside trackway ran east to the shallow point where the river could be forded, which later became Fye Bridge.

What does 'Colegate' mean? Conventional explanations are unconvincing, so I ignore them and opt for something romantic! 'Gate' is easy: it's Danish for 'street' or 'way'. But the meaning of 'Cole' is less certain. I have read, however, that in old English it can mean 'light'. So when, early in the morning, the sun – clear and bright – shines from the east bringing each building to life; and when – in the evening – it shines mellow from the west, turning all it touches to gold, I pretend it means 'the street of light'– perhaps it does!

At the western end of Colegate, at the corner of Oak Street, stands the church or St Michael Coslany, commonly called St Miles. This church is famous for the glorious display of flushwork – decorative patterns of stone and inlaid flint – in the walls of the south aisle, which the artist John Sell Cotman made the subject of one of his engravings. St Miles has been redundant for nearly thirty years, but found a new lease of life as the home of 'Inspire', a hands on science centre. It is surrounded by attractive old houses in St Miles' Alley, including one which was the home of the chantry priest, who was paid to pray for the souls of the departed.

No. 57, Colegate – formerly the Queen Ann – is another of the buildings which give

St George's church, Colegate.

this end of my favourite street its peculiar charm. But only one pub remains in this parish, where once there were many. At the corner of Duke Street, which cut through Colegate when it was constructed early in the nineteenth century, stands the Golden Star, which narrowly escaped demolition in the 1970s, when a drastic road widening scheme was proposed. In fact I nearly demolished the Golden Star in 1969! I hit it with a double-decker bus when road works forced me to mount the pavement. The landlord was very understanding; 'so long as you don't knock the bar down...' was his only comment.

The central section of Colegate lies in the second of the three parishes through which this old street passes: St George, Colegate. Also set on the north side of the street, St George's is a handsome church indeed, with a tower built in 1459 and a nave crowned with an impressive clerestory, which gives the building its distinctive grandeur. The medieval fabric of St George, Colegate houses a superb Georgian interior, with reredos, pulpit with tester and, at the west end, a classical gallery, on which stands the organ: a notable example of the work of George Pike England.

Traces of a consecration cross and other fragments of wall painting – including a beautiful Christ Child on the shoulder of St Christopher – can be seen and a monumental brass of bracket design commemorating William Norwich, mayor in 1461 and Alice, his wife. A set of three mayoral irons, which held the civic sword and maces when the mayor and corporation processed in state, bear the names of eleven eighteenth- and nineteenth-century mayors who lived in this parish.

St George, Colegate is also well known for the unusual terracotta tomb of Robert

The Parish Boundary plates photographed by Jack Burton.

Colegate today by Jack Burton.

Jannys, mayor in 1517 and 1524, whose portrait hangs in Black Friars Hall. Even more importantly, it is the burial place of John Crome, one of England's greatest landscape painters and founder of the Norwich School of Painting.

Facing St George's across the street is a large block of factory buildings, some of which date from early Victorian times. Now restored and converted, these were formerly the home of Howlett and White, one of the leading manufacturers in the days when Norwich was renowned for its boot and shoe industry. When first I moved into Colegate, the smell of leather filled St George's Plain (as this section of the street is known). The radio programme *Music while you Work* blared out for half an hour each morning and afternoon and at leaving off time swarms of shoe hands filled the street as they headed home, many on cycles.

Around St George's, imaginative modern architecture blends happily with much older and traditional styles. Radio Broadland, for example, is housed in a Georgian building, while at the entrance to Muspole Street, beside the churchyard, is the Woolpack, the town house of the Priors of Walsingham in the days when that village was the second most popular place of pilgrimage in England, after Canterbury.

The striking flint building at the east end

of the church, with its west wing in St George's Street (formerly Gildengate) and its east wing in Calvert Street (formerly Snailgate), is Bacon's House, the home of Henry Bacon, a merchant grocer and twice mayor of the city. When the Earl of Warwick visited Norwich in 1549 to crush Kett's Rebellion he lodged here. Bacon's initials and merchant's mark can be seen on the front of the building.

Next to Bacon' s House stand Nos. 27-29 Colegate, charming seventeenth-century houses, with dog-toothed gables. These properties have been restored in recent years. Formerly, No. 29 was Miss Meek's sweet shop. Ruth Meek was a diminutive and well known character, who achieved fame by refusing to yield to the threats of robbers in her shop. Often my son recalls the Saturday evening he called to buy his weekly supply of sherbet lemons. With much puffing Miss Meek climbed some steps to pull down a new jar from a high self. She dropped it and some of the sherbet lemons rolled out all over the floor. He purchased a portion of the few that remained and came away. He claims, however, that over the year which followed he couldn't help noticing that his sherbet lemons from Miss Meek's were always covered with bits of fluff and specks of grit!

Still on the north side of Colegate is the Octagon Chapel, once described by an expert as 'a bout of architectural triumph!' Designed by Thomas Ivory, this exciting building was opened in 1756. It was built by a congregation of Presbyterians who earlier had been ejected from the Church of England when the Act of Uniformity was passed in 1662. They were independent and forthright in their religious opinions and refused to be bullied or browbeaten. This particular congregation became, and remains, Unitarian, rejecting any miraculous element in religion.

The Octagon Chapel is an exuberant expression of classical elegance. Eight giant columns crowned with Corinthian capitals draw the eyes up to the decorated ceiling. Only a few intrepid explorers (and I am one!) have climbed the ladder and passed through the tiny trap door into the dusty, unimaginable world above that beautiful ceiling and seen the octagonal pattern of the timbers that support the roof.

Many famous Norwich citizens have been associated with the Octagon Chapel, which opened its own school. In its heyday it was one of the chief intellectual and social centres in the land – a place of brilliance and wit, which earned it the title of 'the Vatican of the Unitarian hierarchy'. Almost within touching distance of the Octagon Chapel is the Old Meeting House. Moving from one to the other, however, means crossing into the third Colegate parish: St Clement's.

The Old Meeting House is another of Norwich's most special buildings, dating from 1693, and is an important early example of Free Church architecture. It is set back from the street up a narrow alley and was built in what was known formerly as the Friars' Great Garden. The Black Friars, whose church we know as St Andrew's and Blackfriars' Halls, also owned extensive property on the Colegate side of the River. The story of the people who worship at Old Meeting House is a stirring romance of exile, excommunication and covenant. Oppressed by a High Church bishop, a group of local people fled to Rotterdam, returning to form the Norwich and Yarmouth Independent Church and were known later as Congregationalists. Norwich people are not readily overawed by authority! Bishops might order and dictate but in Colegate the independent spirit of the city found expression.

The yard of Old Meeting House is paved with Dutch Clinker; one gravestone mentions Rotterdam and the two doors each contain a round spyhole. Inside, the atmosphere is different from the Octagon. It is

The Octagon Chapel, Colegate.

austere, puritan, peaceful, dignified and powerful. As the clock ticks, the passage of time can be sensed. Between the Octagon and the Old Meeting House is No. 19 Colegate, a seventeenth-century house used today as barristers' chambers. It stands on the boundary of St George's and St Clement's parishes and boasts an interesting set of boundary line-plates. These date from the time when the parishes were the smallest unit of local government and responsible for matters like street cleaning and lighting. It was therefore vital that parish boundaries were marked clearly.

The church of St Clement's at Fye Bridge stands at the Southeast corner of Colegate near to the river, which would have been wider when the first church was built here. St Clement's is part of Viking Norwich and probably one of the oldest ecclesiastical sites in the city. Clement was martyred by being tied to an anchor and thrown in the sea. This is the reason an anchor is featured on the St Clement's boundary line-plates.

St Clement's is a plain and simple little church, but it possesses a vivid and worshipful ambience, which at certain times, particularly in the light of early morning and again in the evening, can become intensely potent. The most famous name associated with this church is Matthew Parker, who has passed into folklore at 'Nosy Parker'. He was Elizabeth I's choice as Archbishop of Canterbury at a critical period in the history of the Church and nation and had remarkable success in maintaining the 'Elizabethan Settlement' holding all wings of the Church of England together at a time of turbulence. As a child his reading master was the priest of St Clement' and his parents are buried beneath the large table-tomb in the churchyard. St Clement's parish is wonderfully unspoiled and contains many notable buildings. No. 30 Colegate, the Merchants Of Colegate, was formerly the Black Boys and it was in the Black Boys Yard that Sarah Glover established the little school at which she taught her Tonic Sol-Fa system of musical notation. John Curwen, a minister from Stowmarket and friend of the minister of the Old Meeting House was introduced to Sarah Glover and subsequently promoted her system.

Nos. 18 and 20 Colegate are noble town houses and both formerly residences of the Harvey family, prominent merchants and bankers. No. 18, occupied by the Broads Authority, has an impressive doorway with a satyr's head keystone. The L-shaped No. 20 has one if the few stone doorways in Norwich and astonishing moulded plasterwork in the ceiling of the rooms fronting the street. Between these and the parish church are the flint remains of a building, which, in 1934, was reconstructed at the Labour Exchange, though it now serves as private offices. In the sixteenth century, however, it was the house of John Aldrich, MP for the city and twice mayor. The date of his second mayoralty, 1570, is carved in the spandrel of the door directly opposite Old Meeting Alley.

In St Clement's Alley stands the Mischief tavern, another imposing flint built sixteenth-century merchant's house. No. 3 Colegate is a beautifully proportioned Georgian house and the home of Jeremiah Ives, mayor in 1769 and 1795. Friars Quay, between Colegate and the River, is a late twentieth-century prize-winning development which has enhanced and repopulated this ancient parish.

So much more could be told! No wonder I feel that Colegate is the best street in the city! Wherever I have lived, I have always made a point of learning something of the history of that area. It makes life more rich and meaningful to be aware of those who created what we have inherited. It belonged to them before it belonged to us! The light of knowledge and understanding enhances our experience of being alive – and Colegate is full of light!

For me Colegate is also full of ghosts: Saxons, Vikings, medieval merchants, Georgian Mayors, weavers, shoe-workers, priests, friars, fervent nonconformists, scholarly men, godly women, school children – an unending pageant which continues to this day. It contains examples of the architectural styles of six centuries, three medieval churches and two of the historic meeting houses of Europe. Not bad for under 500 yards!

Jack Burton

St Andrew's Hall

There are few buildings in Norwich that have had such a long and distinguished history as that of St Andrew's Hall. From its religious origins to its near destruction during the Dissolution, St Andrew's Hall has been put to many uses but has always fulfilled its remit; as an assembly hall for the citizens of Norwich. The Hall began life as a part of a much larger church, the church of St John the Baptist. Originally a Dominican house built on the north side of the River Wensum, it was founded in 1226. Eighty-one years later it was moved to the south side where commencement of the building of the church proper began about 1327 and was completed in 1345.

When that previous church was ravaged by fire in 1413, a new building was erected by the Dominican Friars, the Black Friars and completed in 1471. This was at the expense of no less than Sir Thomas Erpingham (1357-1428), warrior of Agincourt. It is much of that building that survives as we see it today with the present hall occupying what was then the nave. As can be seen by a casual observer, it is constructed largely of flint and stone with brick dressing and lead, slate and pantile roofs. Today it stands as the last surviving building of the four main friaries of medieval Norwich.

Soon after, a dark cloud fell over the future of the church. King Henry VIII was not a man to conform to the rules of convention when he could break them and mould them to his will. Determined to reduce the power of the religious orders and usurp control of the church from the Pope, he set upon this task by dissolving the power of the monasteries. It wasn't long before the new church in Norwich fell prey to his intentions. Faced with possibly the greatest threat in its history, the church was one of those scheduled for destruction in 1538. However, a saviour came forward in the shape of Augustine Steward, the Mayor of Norwich, who fought to persuade the City Corporation to buy the building for the sum of £80. The purpose was to utilise the nave as 'a fayre and large hall, well pathed, for the Mayor and his brethrene, with all the citizens of the same to repair thereunto for their common assembleges as often as shall be expedient.'

St Andrews Hall from the front.

For a brief moment in time, the building's future looked secure. However, just ten years later came another threat to its existence; a rebellion that made famous a man that even today some regard as hero, others a villain. In August 1549, Kett's Rebellion came to town.

The rebellion grew from the frustration of local farmers over the issue of enclosure and land ownership. Small-time landowners were being forced off their land by richer and thus more powerful ones who used enclosure (the containment of their land) to seize larger areas for their own enrichment. Robert Kett, a farmer from Wymondham near Norwich gave the rebellion the leadership it needed and before long, a growing rebel army moved on Norwich.

Empowered to put down the rebel army on behalf of the crown, the Earl of Warwick forced his way into the city on the 24 August 1549 to meet the rebellion head on. His troops brought guns and ammunition into the city but were misdirected and took a wrong turning at Charing Cross, ending up in Bishopgate. It was there that the munitions fell into rebel hands. The rebels had split into three groups earlier on and one of these groups held a position at St Andrew's Hall.

In his attempts to regain control of the situation, Warwick moved his men right into St Andrew's where they immediately came under a hail of arrows fired by the rebels. Luckily for him, a company of musketeers arrived and fired into the rear of the rebel gathering. A fierce battle erupted leaving 300 men dead. The city came under Warwick's control again and St Andrew's Hall became a stable for his army's horses. It remained so until 7 September, 1549 when, the rebellion over, the Royal army left the city

It was the turn of the church and the state to collide in the seventeenth century. The period leading up to the English Civil War was to see much in the way of religious and political strife. The magistrates and councilmen of Norwich controlled the lectureships at St Andrew's and always supported the Puritans. The plain in front of St Andrew's Hall, having once been used as a preaching space by the friars of the hall, was now used for the same purpose by the city itself. It directly challenged the religious authority based at the Cathedral. It was no mere coincidence that the area in front of St Andrew's was called the green-yard after the green-yard in the Cathedral grounds. In an attempt to undermine the authority of the city in 1622, Bishop Harsnett forbade Sunday morning sermons and lectures within the city, apart from those within the Cathedral's jurisdiction. If this was supposed to have brought the local councilmen into line then it met with quiet indifference. Lectures continued in St Andrew's and a dozen influential Norfolk men established a corporation to financially back the admission of Puritan ministers into the city's churches.

Despite all of the trials and tribulations in its history, St Andrew's Hall has been found a purpose in many more peaceful endeavours. According to a city street plaque, the Norwich Mint was housed there between 1696 and 1698 and '£259,371 of silver coinage was struck in this hall by order of King William III.' Two years later, another use had been found. In 1700, the city Corporation set aside a part of the hall to be used as a coffee-house. As well as these uses, the hall also housed various civic functions, as well as being used as the assizes court and as a place for Corporation banquets.

One such banquet had been recorded in 1561. 'Wm Mingay, esq., then Mayor, invited the Earls of Northumberland and Huntingdon, Lords Thomas Howard and Willoughby and many other noblemen and knights, with numerous ladies and gentlemen, to the guild feast, which they accepted and expressed the greatest satisfaction at their generous and hospitable reception. The

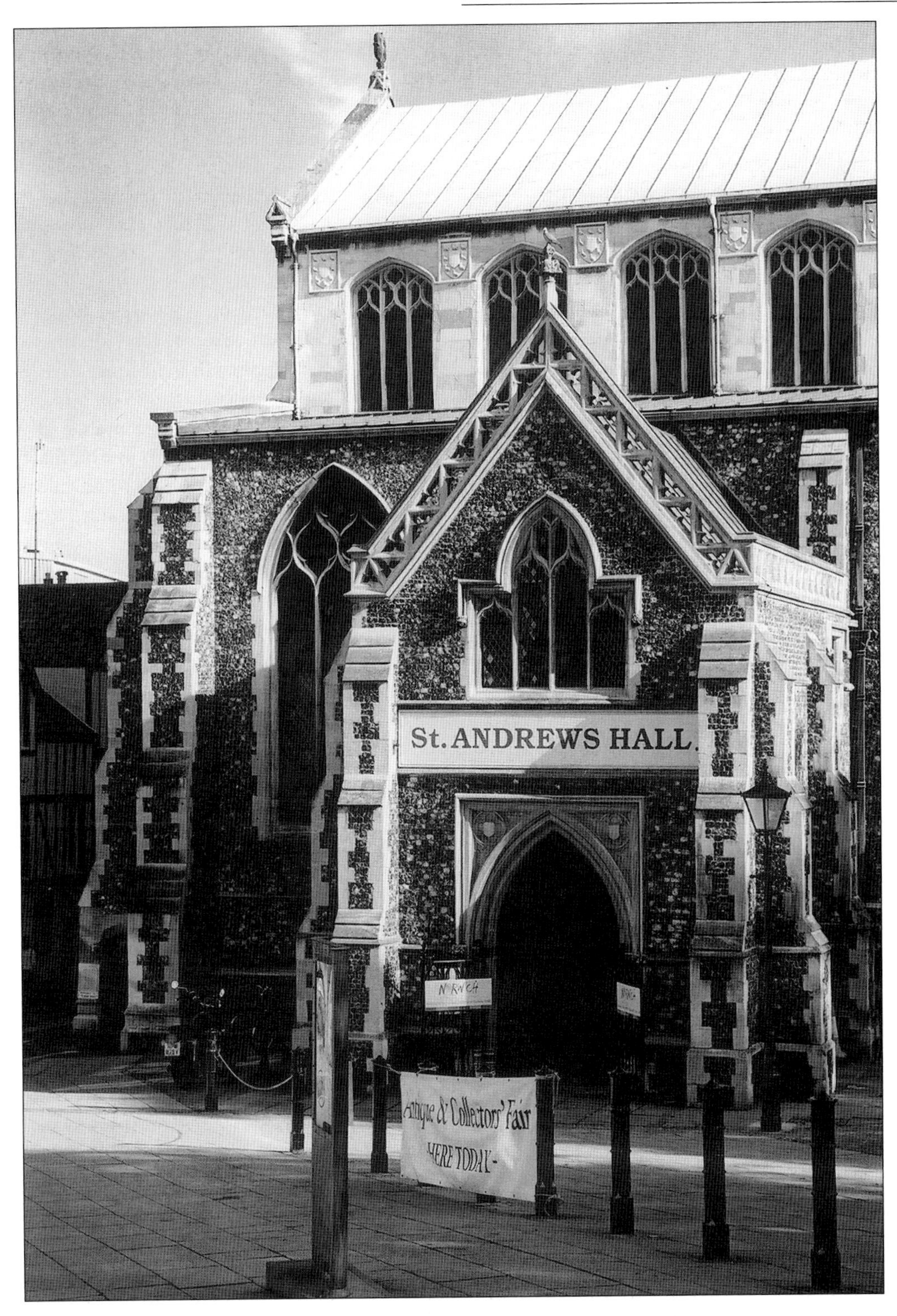

St Andrews Hall.

expense of the feast, according to the bill of fare, amounted to £1 17s 2d.' Almost 250 years later, the hall was still being used as a place for dining. On 25 October 1809, 'the Mayor Thomas Back, esq. invited 341 gentlemen to a roast beef dinner at St Andrew's Hall, which was brilliantly illuminated - a baron of beef weighing 17lb surmounted with the union flag, was brought in by four grenadiers, who carried it twice round and then placed it on top of the table.'

On 18 September 1827, upwards of 350 performers turned up for the 'second grand musical festival for the benefit of the Norfolk and Norwich Hospital' and succeeded in raising £672 12s 1d.

Thirty years previously on 24 October 1798, it had been agreed 'that a request should be made to Lord Nelson to sit for a portrait, to be placed in St Andrew's Hall.' In the 1830 gazetteer of Norwich, one entry reads, 'At the east end is a fine picture, painted by Sir William Beechey, of Admiral Lord Nelson, presented to the corporation in 1804.' If you enter St Andrew's Hall by the main entrance today, turn right and pass through the hall, you will find that the very same painting still hangs in the corridor beyond.

One of the hall's most exciting visitors arrived on the evening of Tuesday 11 October 1859. That most famous Victorian author and public speaker, Charles Dickens, captivated an audience as he read from *A Christmas Carol*, the trial from *Pickwick* and *The Story of Little Dombey and Mrs Gamp*. The stalls cost 4s, the side aisles 2s and the orchestra only 1s. As one man remembering the event in 1913 wrote, 'I was too young to go myself; but what a delightful treat it must have been for those who were old enough to appreciate it!'

In 1774, St Andrew's Hall underwent a major overhaul. Its octagonal tower had already collapsed in 1712. A number of neighbouring buildings were pulled down, the plain was taken in and the city library, housed alongside the hall prior to its move into St Andrew's Street in 1857, was rebuilt over the old gateway. Despite further restoration work carried out in 1863, the building remains largely unchanged today

Amongst other things that take place in the hall now are a regular Antique and Collector's fares and arts and crafts fares. Once a year the hall plays host to the weeklong Norwich Beer Festival. This is organised by the Campaign for Real Ale (CAMRA) and celebrates its twenty-fifth annual festival in 2002. Five hundred and thirty one years after it was built, the hall still carries out the same purpose for which it was saved from Henry VIII's commissioners, as 'a hall to repair unto as a common assembly.'

With £2 million promised (Reported in the *Norwich Citizen* [Norwich City Council], summer 2002) towards further refurbishment of the building, it seems that St Andrew's Hall has many more years of useful service to offer the people of Norwich.

Michael Crouch

Four paintings and a Life Room past

It was important for me to find the right place to study my Fine Art degree. I wanted an attractive but lively city, a building in which I would like to study, somewhere with some history, a good reputation, a large bright space to work in and, most important, access to a life room. Upon entering Norwich School of Art, I had feelings not unlike those recalled by John Brinkley (Principle, 1964-68) when he first came to the art school. 'The moment I walked into this building for the first time, I thought this is exactly how an art school should be' (Marjorie Allthorpe-Guyton with John Stevens, *A Happy Eye, A*

The Norwich School of Art and Design today.

School of Art in Norwich 1845-1982).

I had found a traditional art school that had been running for over 150 years. The building itself had been standing for over a century and offered hints of its past from the layers of paint which coated its lofty, bright studios to the antique figures, once used for drawing exercises and now discarded in the corridors and bar. I especially liked these plaster casts, looking rather the worse for wear but arranged as though standing guard or waiting for something to happen.

Some time in my first year, I came across a painting of the art school by John Wonnacott, *The Norwich School of Art* (1982-4), accompanied by two paintings of the Life Room, one by John Wonnacott (1977-80) and one by John Lessore (1980-81). It was exciting to discover that someone had had a reason to paint the art school at that time and I was inspired by the image of a dedicated and energetic life class depicted in these two, quite different, paintings. I found out that Wonnacott and Lessore had taught at the art school between 1977 and 1986 and I have become increasingly interested in this piece of the art school's past.

In the final year of my degree I made a series of interviews for my thesis, with life models, teachers and students who were involved in the Life Room run by these two artists. There is only a little information about the art school between the '60s and '80s and in a way, I was hoping to fill in the blanks and recover this piece of Life Room past, which I feel is such an important part of the school's history.

In 1871 the Slade School of Fine Art, University College was founded under Poynter, Legros, Brown and Tonks. This began a new concept in life room studies, as these tutors began to teach drawing from the life model. At that time most art schools were still teaching their students to draw purely from anatomical diagrams and antique figures. It was not until the early 1880s that a

Sculptures in the Norwich School of Art and Design. (Courtesy Fine Art Hallways)

life room was introduced at Norwich School of Art. Art students would work from the cast as well as the life model until 1945, when drawing from the antique was finally discontinued. Norwich School of Art was not only late to establish a life room but also slow to reject it.

Lessore and Wonnacott, or the 'Two Johns' as they were called, were asked to run the Life Room at a time when the discipline of life drawing was fading fast in British art schools. It was quite unusual, even at that time, for students to be able to specialise completely in life room studies under full time tuition. The artists even had their own studio spaces in the Life Room and would work alongside their students.

As well as making many paintings of the Life Room over the ten years they spent at the art school, the two Johns also each made a painting of the outside of the building, *The Garth* (1982-3) by John Lessore and *Norwich School of Art* (1982-4), by John Wonnacott. The artists worked on these paintings whilst teaching in the Life Room. These are not merely paintings of the site where both artists taught for so many years and they were not only painted because it was convenient to use the environment they worked in. For the artists they capture some of the essence of the art school at that time and suggest the way they felt about their situation as it was then.

The two paintings of the Life Room, shown earlier, were described by Lynda Morris, friend of the artists and Gallery Norwich Gallery Curator, as 'A metaphor for their concern, as painters and teachers, with the limitation of subject matter that will keep still' (*Marlborough Fine Art*, John Wonnacott: Marlborough Fine Art Catalogue). Lessore and Wonnacott were both taught at the Slade School of Fine Art, where artists such as Henry Tonks, Walter Sickert and William Coldstream passed on to the students a life time's knowledge of painting and drawing, which they had themselves received as students and artists. You could say that the tradition of figurative painting, which these artists came from was as much to do with the desire to teach and to pass on knowledge, as it was with painting itself. This is possibly true for some painters more than others, but I would be surprised if Lessore and Wonnacott had not seen it as their duty to pass on the unique teaching they had themselves

Sculptures in the Norwich School of Art and Design. (courtesy Fine Art Hallways)

been given. So for them, the teaching was more than just a job, in the same way that these paintings were more than just images of the place where they worked. The artists seemed to have a missionary quality and keepers of the torch of the tradition of working from life. I want to use these paintings to transport you back to the period I have been researching and to the art school as my interviewees and the two Johns knew it.

The Garth and *Norwich School of Art* are very different paintings in style, which demonstrates how the two Johns were such different artists in their approach. Wonnacott's paintings are very photographic. This painting, like many others by the artist, has two vanishing points so that an illusion is created. He has taken the view of the building on St George's Street from each side of the road; one point vanishes somewhere near the Red Lion pub, on the right of the picture, and the other vanishes to the left of the picture near the cathedral. The image is curved and the art school building is thrust forward. It towers above the people, along with the rolling sky.

But, for Wonnacott, this is far more than just a painting of the school, as it depicts recognizable characters. There is Bill English, the art school Principal, and Ed Middleditch, Head of Fine Art at that time. Lynda Morris, curator of Norwich Gallery is shown, in conversation with another member of staff on the far right-hand side. A group of students are about to cross the bridge. In the bottom left corner is the artist himself, with his friend and co-worker John Lessore, walking away from the building and about to exit the painting, in a way, a metaphor for their departure from the art school as teachers and, thus, the end of their Life Room. I remember, when I first saw this painting, in the Tate Britain, I was not expecting it to be there and, I suppose, I was so excited to see it because it is something very personal to me. The display caption reads:

Wonnacott taught life drawing there at a time when the discipline was falling out of favour; he was dismissed the year after this painting was completed. Prophetically, he shows himself and two colleagues who left at the same time, in the foreground of the painting, walking away from the building 'like an expulsion from paradise'.

Lessore paints from drawings and, unlike Wonnacott, does not use photographs. *The Garth* depicts a different part of the art school; the courtyard, facing the old monastery that now houses the Visual Studies studios. The painting shows him pushed in the wheelchair by John Wonnacott, mimicking Wonnacott's painting of the front of the building. Some students depart in the right corner of the painting, holding their rulers like candles and walking in procession; somewhat imitating the praying monks which had once walked the grounds. An instant sense of history is attached to the painting, from the ruins of the monastery to the muted tones and painterly qualities, reminiscent of paintings by Sickert and Degas. In this painting the composition is brought together through the rhythm of the paint, in the unity of colour and tone and the repetition of motifs throughout, like the vertical and horizontal lines which make up the stone on the ground, fences and posts, the construction of the building and the rulers held in the foreground. There is an element of narrative to the painting as Lessore tells an imaginative story of history, people and a place. It is painted with affection. The earnest figures in front betray the attitude of his dedicated Life Room students.

This romantic tone follows into Lessore's painting, *The Life Room, Norwich*, as he

Main entrance to the Norwich School of Art and Design.

depicts what is, to him, an ideal situation. The characters are unrecognisable; however its sister painting, *The Life Room*, by John Wonnacott, can be seen in the distant background, where it was being worked on at the time. The composition is, once again, unified through repeated gestures, more now from the curves of the figures, as it is difficult to tell the plaster casts apart from the students. They become enchanting presences, watching over the group with the authority of their past use. I learnt that Lessore restored these antiques himself during his time at the art school. In my opinion, this is the most beautiful of the four paintings. It presents an idealised perception of the Life Room.

Wonnacott's painting is a more realistic impression of the Life Room and Wonnacott shows it set up as it was. The partition for third and second year students to work in can be made out at the back of the room, behind the model. Prints by four major Post Impressionists: Van Gogh, Cézanne, Gaugin and Seurat that the artist put up himself can be seen on the right hand wall, on the right of Ed Middleditch, who is standing as though he has just come in to take a look at what is going on. The students in this painting are all recognisable characters and the artist himself can just be made out on the far left hand side next to an antique cast and behind Lessore's painting which is enclosed in the space he built to work in. Lessore himself, in the foreground, thoughtfully observes. Writing about this painting in an exhibition catalogue, Wonnacott says:

I am fascinated by the theatre of the Life Room in all its artificialit... The students recorded in this painting are from among those young painters who, with a particular commitment to and/or talent for perceptual drawing, have made regular use of the Life Room during my... years at Norwich. (Richard Morphet, *The Hard-Won Image, Traditional Method and Subject in Recent British Art)*

Wonnacott paints the functional Life Room, with all its necessary equipment, the prints on the wall, a skeleton for demonstration and a backdrop and heaters for the model, who is in a rigid, seated position. All this shows his fascination with the technical side of drawing. Lessore's Life Room may not be such a truthful description of how it really looked, as he has been selective of detail, however this painting is more descriptive of the way the artist felt about the magic of the Life Room. Lessore has used artistic licence in this painting, in the same way that his other works flow with expression and imagination. There is a mystical atmosphere to his Life Room as well as a feeling of antiquity that reflects Lessore's concern for the history behind this discipline. Calmness passes over this room, as the students, painted with such affection, work away peacefully and the model appears almost to be sleeping.

All four paintings of the Art School are magnificent works, which would not have existed without the Life Room. Lessore and Wonnacott left the art school in 1986 after a disagreement with the new head of Fine Art, over changes that were to be made to the life room. Attempts were made to liven it up and introduce new tutors, as it was seen as a cosy, sleepy place and Wonnacott and Lessore's objections lead to their dismissal. Ever since then, the Life Room at Norwich has gradually vanished, which brings us to the present day where there is no space for a permanent life room at all.

Nowadays, in the absence of a life room at Norwich, life drawing is currently held a block away from the Fine Art studios on St George Street and is only an option as a means of study on one day a week. Students are not offered any sort of tuition within the Life Room, which I personally believe to be a great loss. As British art schools are changing and life rooms all over the country disappearing, I see an obvious reason to look back with appreciation to this past tradition in British painting and a way of learning which is no longer accessible from the modern art school. The antique casts that I have found so appealing ever since I first came to the art school, have been a constant reminder to me of the Life Room which no longer exists. As guardian angels of the School, I can only imagine that they are watching and waiting patiently for a revival of the Life Room.

Josephine Jenkins

Cathedral church of St John the Baptist

St John's stands on a commanding site to the west of the city. It is the Roman Catholic Cathedral of the Diocese of East Anglia. The building of the cathedral commenced in 1882 and was completed in 1910. At that time it was of course not a cathedral at all. Norwich was part of the Roman Catholic Diocese of Northampton and this church was built as the parish church for the Roman Catholics of Norwich. It became a cathedral in 1976 when the three counties of Norfolk, Suffolk and Cambridgeshire were formed into the Diocese of East Anglia. The church was the gift of Henry Fitzalan Howard, 15th Duke of Norfolk who at the age of thirty had married Lady Flora Hastings. Shortly after that time the idea came to him that he would build a church as an act of thanksgiving to God for his happy marriage and he decided to build it in Norwich. The architect of the church was George Gilbert Scott. He was the son of Gilbert Scott, one of the most prolific of English Victorian architects. Several possible sites for the church were considered. The one finally chosen had previously been occupied by the city gaol. The style of the building is thirteenth-century Gothic. In Victorian times, in the Gothic Revival, medieval work was copied. Duke Henry and George Gilbert Scott noted that among the great number of medieval churches to be seen in Norwich none had survived the rebuilding of the Decorated and Perpendicular periods and so none represented to the Early English phase of Gothic. That is what they tried to achieve in St John's.

The building has many fine features. Striking is the magnificent rood beam with the wooden painted Calvary. The figure of Christ was carved by Peter Rendle who was well known as one of the principal players in the Oberammergau Passion Play. Also noteworthy are the carvings, the grey Frosterley marble and of course the windows, which are regarded by the experts as some of the finest nineteenth-century stained-glass windows in Europe. With the exception of the Walsingham Chapel, whose windows are by Clayton and Bell, all the windows were designed and executed by the form of John Hardman & Co. of Birmingham. The green windows, called grisaille work, are a feature of the building; each one has a unique pattern. After the north side windows were blown out in the war, the high clerestory windows were moved down to replace them and new clear clerestory windows were put in to give more light. The masons followed the medieval custom of carving faces, possibly their colleagues or notable citizens of the time – we will never know – although two heads in the nave are said to represent Cardinals Newman and Manning.

The Stations of the Cross, marking the stages of Christ's journey to Calvary were installed in 1971 by Mgr McBride and were carved by Ferdinand Stufflesser of Ortisei, Italy. A copy of the painting of Our Lady of Czestochowa marks the memorial to the

St John's Catholic Church under construction, pre-1910.

Polish men and women who died in the Second World War. The painting was blessed by Pope John Paul II when he visited the United Kingdom in 1982. The statue of St Anthony of Padua was given by Miss O'Riorden who lived in Heigham Grove.

The large doorway in the north transept was originally one of the main entrances to the church. For the year 2000 it was the special Holy or Jubilee Year Door. 'Holy Year' is the name given to a year in which the Catholic faithful are invited to make a special pilgrimage to Rome, while those who cannot do so are given the opportunity of making visits to designated churches in their own diocese. St John's was a designated church and so had its own Holy Door.

The window in the north transept is known as The Queen's Window or the Pilgrimage Window. The original glass was destroyed in the Second World War but has been restored in accordance with the original design, which had been kept safely by John Hardman & Co. of Birmingham. In the centre is depicted Our Lady enthroned, holding the Christ Child. In the three groups above are types of Our Lady, Judith, Queen Esther and the Queen of Sheba parting with Solomon. The whole theme of this window is Our Lady presenting Christ to the world.

To the right of this window is the apsidial chapel (modelled on a chapel in the cathedral at Laon) is dedicated to Our lady of Walsingham. In this chapel is to be found a carved and painted gilt wooden statue and reredos. The traditional figure of Our Lady of Walsingham is in the altarpiece. The original windows were erected in 1909, having been designed by the second Duchess (the Hon. Gwendolen Harries). The left-hand window shows at the top of the original vision of Richeldis de Favarches. While spending a night in prayer she had a vision of the Virgin Mary and was told to build a replica of the Holy House at Nazareth. We see her vision and angels holding the Holy House. In the centre we see Geoffrey de Favarches, son of Richeldis and the building of the Priory. Below is shown a pilgrimage to the shrine by the Duke and Duchess of Norfolk who are shown with the others starting from the Slipper Chapel having left their footwear behind in order to walk the last mile barefoot. In the centre at the top we have Our Lady, enthroned and crowned with a sceptre of lilies and holding the Holy Child upon her knee. In the centre, in the lower part of the window we see Queen Catherine (the first wife of Henry VIII) giving thanks for the victory of Flodden Field in 1513. To the right of Queen Catherine kneels the victor of Flodden – Thomas Howard, Earl of Surrey, later to become the 2nd Duke of Norfolk. To the right at the top we see pilgrims at the Holy Well. The burning of the statue at Chelsea during the Reformation can be seen. Below we see the restoration of the Catholic shrine at the Slipper Chapel in 1934 with Cardinal Bourne and Bishop Youens. The squirrel is a reference to Mgr Harold Squirrell who was rector of St John's at the time.

The aisle to the north of the sanctuary forms a chapel that in 1984 was dedicated as a Chapel of Prayer for Christian Unity. The icon of Jesus Christ, Pantocrator, Lord of All was dedicated and erected by Bishop Alan Clark at a Unity Service in January 1984. The bible was given by Canon Frank Millet, taken from the redundant church of St John de Sepulchre in 1984.

The chancel at the east end of the cathedral consists of four bays raised a few feet above the nave. A slightly later architectural style has been adopted here, with richer mouldings and carvings. The Bishop's Chair (his cathedra – the origin of the word cathedral) stands against one of the pillars. The High Altar was originally situated against the east wall with the tester (canopy) above. To conform to the liturgical

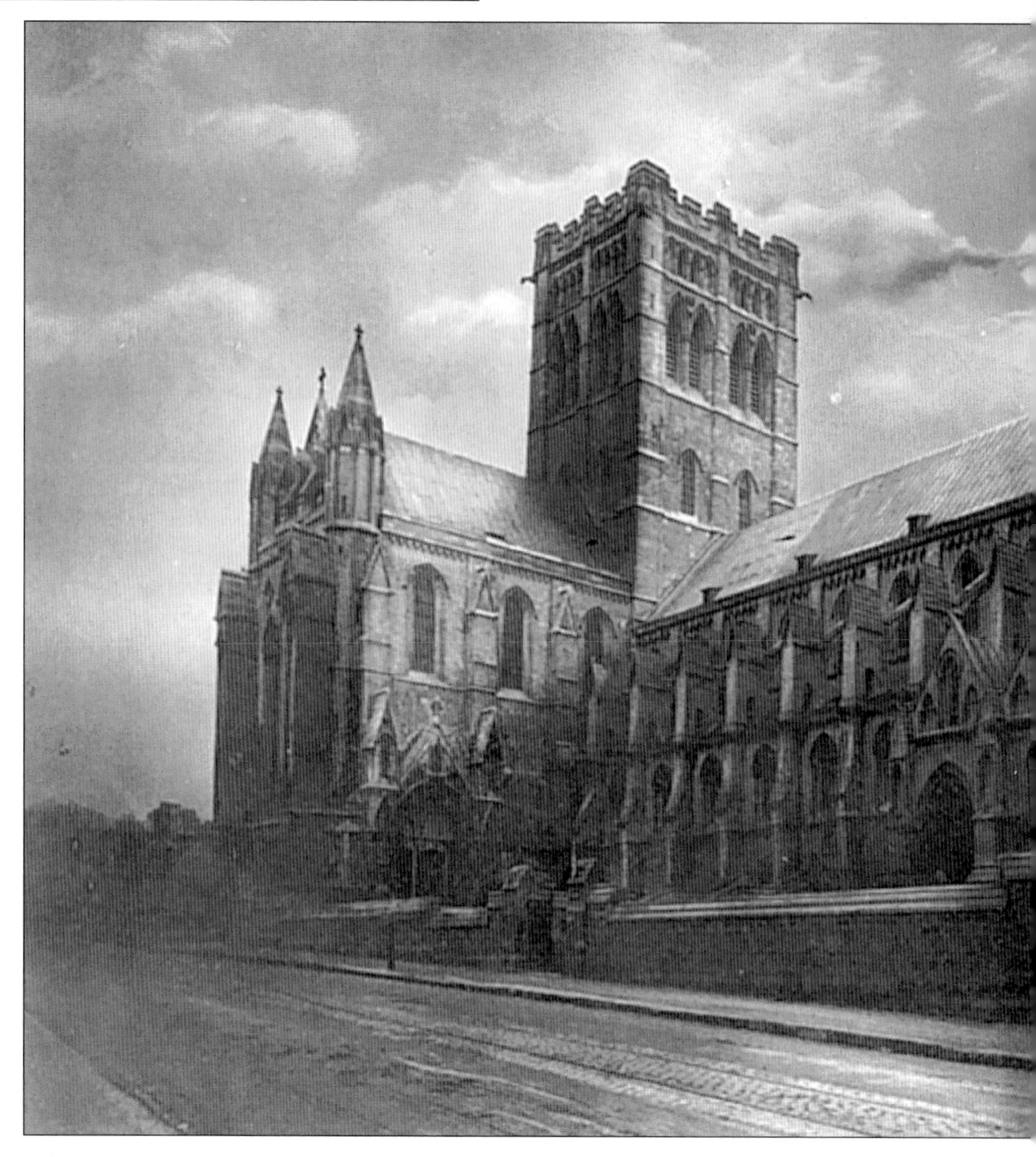

The completed St John's Catholic Church.

reforms of the Second Vatican Council in the 1960s the present altar was constructed (using the top is the original high altar and some of the marble and stonework) and placed much closer to the people. Three large pictures of the secondary patrons of the Diocese (the principal patron is Our Lady of Walsingham) were in 2000 erected on the east wall, from left to right, St Felix, St Ethelreda and St Edmund. They were painted by a local artist, Becky Nelson.

The theme of the east window is the creation, redemption and sanctification of man. To the left we find the Eternal Father.

Below is a representation of the Immaculate Conception in the mind of the Father. The top centre window shows the Council of the Holy Trinity. The panel beneath shows Christ the High Priest and victim stepping down from the throne. At the base we see the birth of Bethlehem. The bottom centre shows the Sacrifice on Calvary. Adam stands at the foot of the tree of redemption receiving the precious blood. The circles below show the betrayal, Our Lord giving himself up willingly. Also illustrated are the guards at the sepulchre from which rises the glorified figure of Our Lord. To the right at the top we see the Holy Spirit moving on the face of the waters and below, the Annunciation with, in adjoining circles, angels adoring the God made Man. At the bottom the medallion represents the Birthday of the Church.

The south aisle of the chancel has always been the Blessed Sacrament Chapel. On the altar is situated the Tabernacle in which the Blessed Sacrament is reserved. The red sanctuary lamp, formerly in the chapel of the Convent of the Little Sisters of the Assumption, is kept burning as a sign that the Blessed Sacrament is reserved in the tabernacle.

The chapel at the east end of the south transept contains a memorial for the men of the parish who died in the First World War. The altar cross was originally on the old High Altar.

In the south transept are to be found the confessionals and, above them, the Dukes' Gallery. The window above the confessionals depicts the birthday of the church. We see the events of Pentecost with figures descending bearing scrolls. Below are the twelve Apostles portrayed as Bishops, with mitres and tongues of fire. St Peter in the centre bears keys in his left hand, with a throne behind him and his right hand raised, a figure of commanding certainty and authority.

The chapel leading from the south aisle is commonly known as the Sunk Chapel as its level is lower than that of the nave. It has at various times been known as the Lady Chapel, the Memorial Chapel and St Joseph's Chapel. The windows comprise a memorial to Lady Flora. Each one represents

St John's Cathedral today.

Norwich Castle entrance.

one of her Christian names – Flora, Pauline, Esther and Barbara. It contains the statues of St Joseph and Our Lady, by Ferdinand Stufflesser. On the walls of the aisle are the arms of the 15th Duke in dried material by Mrs B. Kemp of Sheringham. The arms of Howard and Hastings appear in windows in and adjoining this chapel. At the west end of the aisle is the Pieta.

The gallery was originally intended for the organ. This was partly built, but never completed because of lack of funds. In 1999 the old Maddermarket organ was being checked to see whether it could be sold. In the documentation with that organ, papers were found indicating that the partly built original organ had been sold by the makers to the Royal Household and was installed in the Chapel of Whitehall Palace. Further research revealed that the instrument was subsequently installed in a chapel in the Tower of London. Eventually it was removed and the pipe work was stored at Hampton Court. The Royal Household was contacted and we were informed that HM the Queen had agreed that St John's could have the organ pipes free of charge.

The great west window represents St John the Baptist pointing out the Messiah. In the centre light is Christ on the cross surrounded by the four greater prophets, with King David and Malachy. Above is the Holy Spirit in the form of a dove and in the apex the Eternal Father in glory. Below is John the Baptist, pointing to Christ with the words 'Behold the Lamb of God'.

This church, besides its role as the cathedral church of the Diocese of East Anglia, is the focus of a thriving parish covering the southern part of the City of Norwich.

Peter Warrington

Norwich Castle

The history of Norwich Castle dates back to 1067 when the Normans built the first wooden fort. The stone keep has been many things, royal residence, 'police station', prison and museum.

During its incarnation as a prison people condemned to death by hanging were executed in public from the castle walls. The death was protracted and so if a prisoner came from a rich family a city urchin would have been paid 1d to hang from the prisoner's legs. This added weight would snap the condemned man's neck and thus hasten the end...

Sarah Skinner

The Ethelbert Gateway

There are two entrances to the Norwich's Anglican cathedral and the Ethelbert Gate is the older and more ornate. The people of Norwich built it in 1272 as a penance. In the Middle Ages the Norwich market place was located in front of the cathedral and large taxes had to be paid to the monks within the Cathedral Close. When the taxes were raised again, the market traders revolted and sent flaming arrows into the Close to show their upset. In doing so they burned down the wood and thatch church of St Ethelbert. The Bishop of Norwich was not happy with this and decreed that the people had to build the gateway in repentance. The middle floor of the gateway is a consecrated chapel that the monks used instead of a church. Incidentally, the Bishop of Norwich raised the taxes anyway!

Sarah Skinner

Ethelbert gate, Norwich Cathedral.

Erpingham Gate, Norwich Cathedral, pre-1918.

The Erpingham Gateway

This entrance to the Cathedral is named for Sir Thomas Erpingham – a local hero long before Admiral Lord Nelson. Sir Thomas led the English archers to victory over the French at Agincourt in 1415. Erpingham is depicted on the gateway kneeling in prayer and his story was immortalised by William Shakespeare in his play *Henry V*.

Sarah Skinner

Cow Tower, c. 1904.

Cow Tower

Originally Cow Tower was built as part of the city's defences along the riverbank and is a fourteenth-century, free standing brick tower.

The name derives from a probable urban myth. It is said that one day a cow wandered into the tower whilst grazing in the area. The cow managed to climb to the top of the tower, but was unable to come down...

Sarah Skinner

6 Highdays and Holidays

Spartan holidays in Brundall

Some of the most noteworthy holidays we ever spent were at our holiday chalet at Brundall, on the River Yare. We had bought this chalet before moving from Wroxham back to Surrey, to keep a link with Norfolk.

The Brown family would set off very early, for a drive of at least four hours. It was a carload of differing views and expectations. Father, Bill, was happy to be returning to the fishing and boating activities he had always loved. Mother, Ida, enjoyed touring in the country, but had a fear of water. For an unknown reason, dinghies with red sails terrified her – something in her childhood perhaps. Nevertheless, she went along with the plans. I, Barbara, the elder daughter, loved the life; the younger, Margaretta, was not so keen.

The journey from Croydon to Norfolk always seemed endless and we hated it. The car would be loaded with necessities and Margaretta and I were cramped in the back seat, sitting on folded blankets, with a large carton of groceries between us. We were not

Relaxing by the chalet at Brundall.

Boating at Brundall.

good travellers and every such trip was fraught with frequent stops. A 'steady 50 mph' was the speed Bill thought best, despite pleas to go a little faster. Margaretta and I even invented a game to help him. He'd be given ten points and every car he overtook would gain him a point and he would lose a point each time we were overtaken. But he'd never play and his points went down to zero very quickly! We'd usually revert to singing in an effort to pass the time. Reading of course was strictly forbidden.

The day before setting off, Bill would spread his map on a table and study it for at least an hour. Then he'd fold it, saying, 'Right – I've decided on our route.' He never made any notes, nor did he refer to the map again. Only occasionally would he take a wrong turn and lengthy post mortems would be held later. Usually these were along the line of 'I almost took the "such-and-such" road, but just then "someone" did "something" to distract me.' Ida anticipated this and would say laughingly 'I wondered how long it would be before it was my fault!'

Eventually we'd arrive at Brundall, and take the narrow road with its high banks that lead to the railway station and level crossing. If the gates were closed, our impatience was unbearable, especially as they were operated manually. The railway man would deal with one gate at a time, in a very leisurely manner. The steam engines seemed huge and would huff and puff very noisily, emitting a wonderful – to us – smell. Once past, we at last arrived at No. 4, Riverside. The narrow road was compacted earth and potholes and had begun life as a quiet towpath, with plots allocated for recreation only. Building had not been permitted, however, gradually the fishing umbrellas left up became tarpaulin hovels, then more durable shelters were built, until eventually a variety of chalets came into being.

Describing our holiday home as a chalet is an exaggeration. An enlarged garden shed would be more accurate. It was divided into two rooms, one of which converted to a bedroom at night. The windows were depressingly small. Outside by the hedge was a hefty wooden shelf, on which rested a calor gas ring and an enamel washing up bowl. This we called the kitchen – there was a narrow roof that gave slight shelter, but only when the rain was straight and heavy. The fridge was a round hole in the ground with a wooden lid and kept the food perfectly fresh. The earth was more black shingle than soil and very wet, so a brick was positioned in the bottom of the fridge to lift the milk and butter out of water. On the other side of the chalet, almost hidden under a tall privet hedge was an Elsan chemical toilet – don't think about it!

There was running water too – from an old iron pump, less than half a mile down the path. It only took about ten minutes to reach the pump, where Margaretta and I pumped energetically in order to fill two heavy water cans. We used to carry them slung on an oar. The weight and difference in our height made the journey back much slower. Fetching water was a great feature of these holidays. This pump was only yards from the river, but the water came from far below the river bed (we hoped) and was said to be fit for babies to drink. It certainly had a wonderful taste, which I can only describe as metallic. (Many years later, on a nostalgic visit, I found this old pump lying in the bushes. On a subsequent visit it had vanished).

The lack of electricity didn't bother us much either. We had two small oil lamps and soon got used to carrying them around – the light didn't reach very far. Candles we kept for emergencies. Anyway, the evenings were light almost until we went to bed, tired after our busy days in the fresh air. When the weather was wet, we happily played board and card games, or went out, maybe to Norwich, to visit the Cathedral and Castle.

Naturally we wore old comfortable clothes, although the casual wear of today did not exist for men. There is a photograph of Bill, taken only a few years before, holding an enormous pike he had caught in the dyke at the end of the house in Wroxham, in which he is wearing a three piece suit and a tie. One day Margaretta decided she wanted to wear a skirt and pretty top, rather than the jeans and jumper Ida had produced. Neither would give way – Ida put the better clothes out of sight, and so Margaretta stayed in bed all morning. Eventually she had to give in and appeared in the holiday clothes at lunchtime.

In a fit of extravagance, a Tilley Lamp was acquired. This gave a wonderfully bright light, especially when compared to the dim yellow of the oil lamps. The Tilley lamp did have one disadvantage – Bill was the only one able to light it. As most people know, the gas mantle had to be lit, and then a pump on the base used. The timing was tricky and getting it wrong, would result in a large blue/yellow flame, instead of a neat white light. The rest of us failed week after week, despite demonstrations, explanations and eventually exasperated lectures. After his fishing trips, Dad would come rowing homeward up the Yare at dusk, guided to the chalet by the flaring lamp, which we'd placed at the end of the jetty. We were inside, sitting round a candle, waiting for him.

Our plot had a 40ft frontage onto the Yare, where the river was particularly wide. A little jetty jutted out in the centre, with dinghies, one with an outboard motor, moored each side. It was such a pleasure to row up and down the river, admiring the houseboats and chalets on our side and enjoying the scenery on the other. The rule was that, when alone, we should not go out of sight round either bend, but as this gave us a very large varied area, it didn't matter. One of the landmarks was Coldham Hall, a public house on the opposite bank downstream. The landlord at the time of the Second World War bore a remarkable likeness to Sir Winston Churchill. The American service men stationed in Norfolk would queue up to buy him a drink and have a photograph taken with him. The pictures were no doubt sent back home with some impressive story.

On the opposite bank were tall trees, behind which was Surlingham Broad, the marshy area all around being a nature reserve. A narrow dyke led into the Broad and we loved our slow quiet trips there, seeing the birds at close range. There were grebe, coots, moorhens and herons. In spring we'd glide past many nests. We particularly liked the grebes with their attractive neck ruff and were fascinated at the distance they travelled under water. Other birds, faint specks in the far distance were pointed out – we usually pretended to see them. The bittern still inhabited the area in those days and we often heard its distinctive boom. The broad, fringed with reeds and inaccessible from the land, had a row of sunken boats along one side. Many of these were wherries from bygone days and we felt the nostalgia that their days were over. At one time, these wherries would travel into the broad and out again by the far dyke, thereby cutting off a large bend in the river. Now the water was shallow and I remember one

Brundall church.

occasion when we were stuck on the mud with the tide going out and our father only just managed to push off in time. I was so worried that we'd have to wait twelve hours for the tide to come in again and our mother, (probably still battling with the Tilley lamp) would be in a state of panic.

The Yare was noticeably tidal and on exceptional occasions rose and flooded the lawn. Fortunately the chalet was high enough to escape the water –we had a very large toad living underneath and fancied that he/she was tame. At least, he crawled out regularly in the same place and would accept worms from us.

Large cargo boats would pass slowly by on their way to Norwich. They were so huge. The first one we saw will always stay in my memory, it was *Jim M*. I saw it approaching from downstream, where it didn't look alarmingly large, but as it slowly came nearer, it grew enormous. Eventually it passed by, blocking the whole of the river from our view and towering above the plot. It was painted black. The sailors always waved in a very friendly way as they passed by. Later came *Mary M* and others, but we referred to them as *Jim M*s ever after. One evening a *Jim M* came upstream at dusk and for some reason moored across the bend in the river by the Yare Hotel and halfway across our frontage. Next morning, there it was, looking extremely threatening. Out in the dinghy one day, Ida in the stern with Bill rowing, he saw one approaching from behind, but didn't say so, knowing that Ida would be terrified. The ship was almost upon us before she heard the low thrum of the engine and looked round, then up, Oh horrors! Another time, Bill was almost crushed by one as he rowed along by the reeds on a bend. We grew very fond of these ships, and looked forward to seeing them.

At the time we had the chalet, the land on the other side of the road was open – a wide space with dykes threading through it and a wooden bandstand in the centre – somewhat puzzling. There were towpaths to walk and fallen trees in the marsh to climb on. During our time there the first land was acquired for new boatyards and we were horrified when fences appeared. These we ignored for as long as possible and continued playing there. Finally we were told firmly to keep out of 'private property' – Private? It was ours!

After a few years of the extremely spartan conditions, Bill enlarged the chalet. Single handedly he built two rooms, a large one for eating and sitting and a smaller one for a kitchen – luxury, although we still had to fetch water and the sink outlet merely emptied into a bucket beneath. It certainly made all the difference, especially for the parents who no longer needed to turn the living area into a bedroom each night.

We had many happy holidays here, but eventually began to outgrow the activities. One day, a man stopped to ask directions to another property, which he was hoping to buy. Bill's reply was 'Want to have a look at mine?' and the answer was 'I'll take it.' This was very rash, as there was a tall hedge in front of the chalet and this conversation was taking place in the chained off parking area in front. He could not have had any idea of what he had bought. Nevertheless the transaction was completed and No. 4 Riverside was sold for £400!

Barbara Brown (Coulsdon resident)

Sunday school treats

I was born at Horsham St Faiths in 1938. The house, in Blind Lane, had a thatched roof, with Virginia creeper growing on the walls. When I was four and a half, I started attending the village primary school, which is still in use today. I was taken by my brother and still remember the sound my feet made in

The chapel at St Faith's where Molly Burton went to Sunday school.

the scraper as we went in through the porch. The vicar visited most weeks, as it was a Church school.

I don't remember exactly how it happened, but when I was about six I started going to Sunday school at the chapel, which was Methodist. It was held in what was called the schoolroom – a neat wooden hall beside the chapel which was only demolished about three years ago (1999).

Mr Woodcock, the thatcher, taught the older children and Mrs Harrod, (usually called Aunt Polly), taught the infants. Two old gentlemen, Mr Pointer and Mr Taberham, sat either side of a small table at the front and a large hymn sheet hung from the ceiling. Mr Taberham sometimes told us a story, as did Mrs Young, the village postmistress, who also often attended. Altogether, I think there were about seventy children. Halfway through, Mrs Harrod took the infants out to the chapel vestry for their lesson. We all enjoyed singing the hymns and choruses.

Once, on the way to Sunday school, I found my younger sister waiting for Mrs Vincent, who gave us rides in her milk-cart, so I took her along with me. My mother wasn't too pleased because my sister didn't have her best clothes on!

Each year, Mr Moore from the Caravan Mission to Village Children would attend our Sunday school. He would be there every evening for a week, telling us interesting stories. We each had a little card that was clipped each evening to mark our attendance and perhaps we would be given a coloured text. Sometimes, Mrs Harrod took children to hear Mr Moore at a rally in St Andrew's Hall, in Norwich. Mrs Harrod also ran a club for children called the Sunshine Club, to which we went each week and played games. She always made sure everyone got home safely.

We had wonderful Christmas parties, with sandwiches, cakes and jellies set out on long trestle tables and silent movies as the evening's entertainment. In the summer time we went to Yarmouth on the Sunday School outing, usually needing four coaches to accommodate the children and also many parents. These were hired from Broadland coaches.

The Sunday School Anniversary was a very important occasion, especially for the girls as we all had new dresses and our mums and dads came to hear us sing and say recitations. The Anniversary was held in the lovely old chapel – which has a balcony all the way round – twice on the Sunday and repeated again on the Monday evening. (This didn't please my mother, as she was tired, probably after washing all day). When I was older I began going to the chapel services regularly. Each quarter, a plan was published of the preachers who were coming to the chapel, which we studied carefully because we liked some more than others! Along with some friends, I joined the choir. We sat at the front of the chapel. We used to practice in the vestry on Friday evenings.

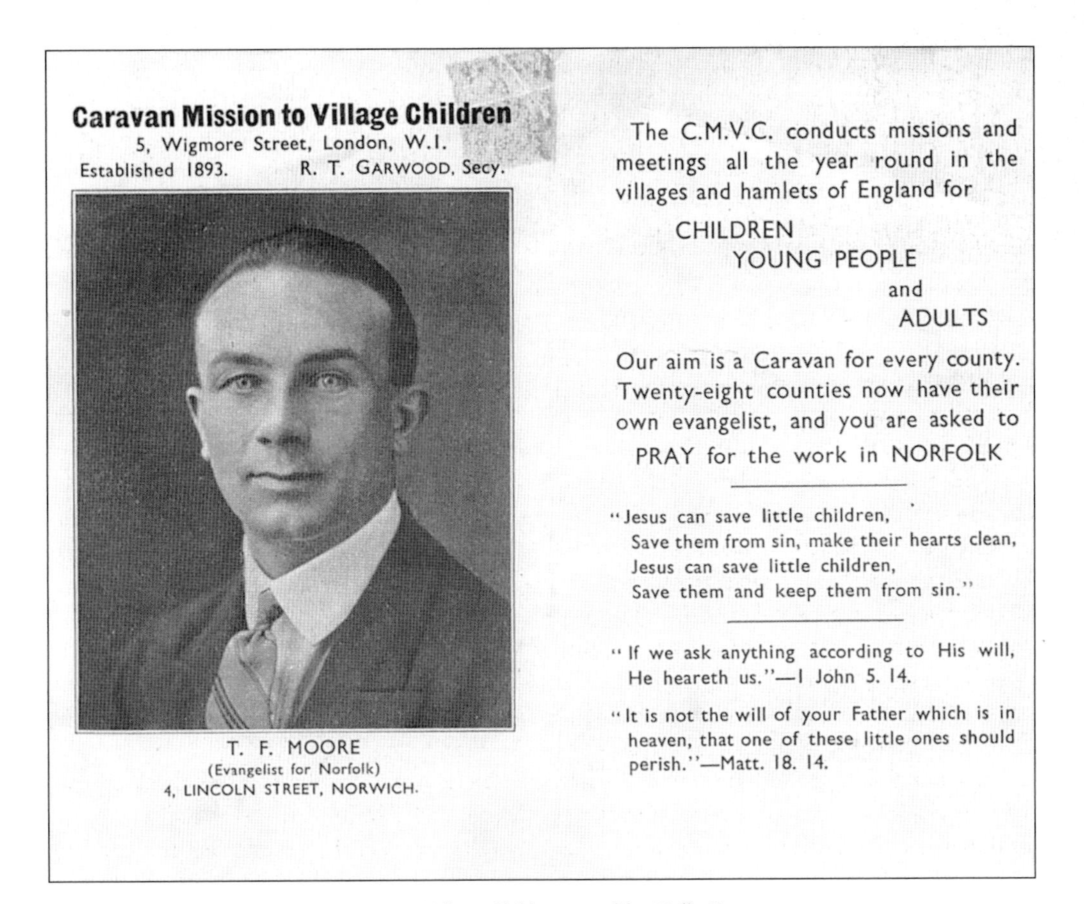

Caravan Mission to Village Children
5, Wigmore Street, London, W.I.
Established 1893. R. T. GARWOOD, Secy.

T. F. MOORE
(Evangelist for Norfolk)
4, LINCOLN STREET, NORWICH.

The C.M.V.C. conducts missions and meetings all the year round in the villages and hamlets of England for

CHILDREN
YOUNG PEOPLE
and
ADULTS

Our aim is a Caravan for every county. Twenty-eight counties now have their own evangelist, and you are asked to PRAY for the work in NORFOLK

"Jesus can save little children,
Save them from sin, make their hearts clean,
Jesus can save little children,
Save them and keep them from sin."

"If we ask anything according to His will, He heareth us."—I John 5. 14.

"It is not the will of your Father which is in heaven, that one of these little ones should perish."—Matt. 18. 14.

A programme from the Caravan Mission to Village Children, saved by Molly Burton.

A Sunday school outing photograph from Molly Burton's album.

Sometimes, I wanted to go out for the evening, so the choirmaster compromised and let me go at eight thirty. We used to lead the hymn singing and provide an anthem. Sometimes we sang at other chapels; we often went to Newton St Faiths.

At the Harvest Festival, we had a harvest supper on the Saturday evening, when the men served the food. The chapel was decorated for the Sunday services, when the choir sang anthems like 'Ho! Reapers in the whitened harvest.' Finally, an auction of the fruit and vegetables was held on the Monday evening.

At Christmas, the choir went carol singing, which we really enjoyed. Mr Woodcock carried a Tilley-lamp on a long stick so that we could see where we were going as we made our way around the darkened village. I remember stopping for mince pies at Mrs Young's house.

Eventually, I did a little Sunday school teaching and helped to set up and run a Girls Life Brigade. I became friendly with one of

Molly married the preacher in 1961.

the younger preachers who visited the chapel. We became engaged and were married at the chapel on a hot Midsummer's day in 1961.

Molly Burton

How the mighty (Utd) were fallen!
Prize-winning entry

My mother said I was always a 'kicker'. For the whole nine months and a bit more, she swore I always kicked. I should've been born in June, but thankfully I arrived a week or so late, saving me from the humiliation of being christened June or worse still, Rosebud! What kind of names would they have been for a footballer in 1946, even though I was a girl?

I grew up living in the house attached to the petrol station that my father owned, on Dereham Road. It was sandwiched between The Earl of Leicester pub and a row of small shops including a fish and chip shop, where for an armful of newspapers you could get a free bag of chips. Next to that was a small general store, run by Miss Brown and Mildred and then came Keith Hansell's dad's cobblers shop. 'Enterprise Garage,' our sign said,

Diane's father's petrol station.

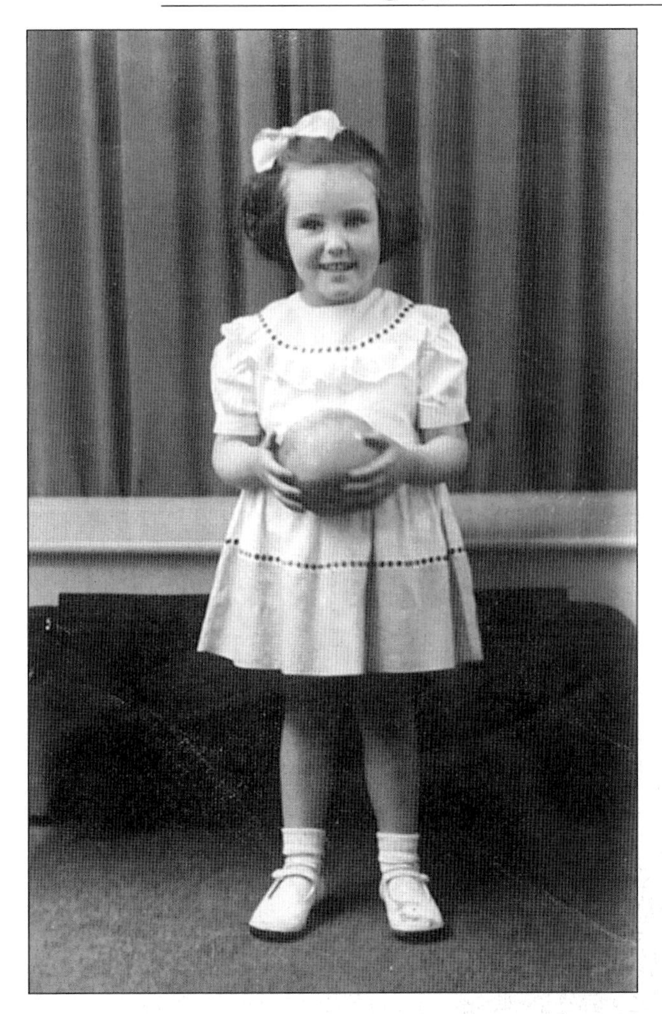

'Footie mad' and only four years old.

'Petrol, Car and Bicycle Repairs'.

Our back garden was bounded by our outhouse, the garage workshop with its row of ball-magnetic windows and a tall corrugated-iron fence that had a wooden bench underneath. My brother and I used to climb up onto this bench, in order to see and communicate with the children who lived on the other side, at the bottom of Bowthorpe Road, opposite the cemetery. We used to stand there for ages, singing songs together, first finger-joints, noses and eyes all that was visible of us from their side. Our favourite at the time was 'Hey, Mr Porter' because a real live Mr Porter lived opposite us on the Dereham Road and he kept a real live horse and cart. Occasionally we would see Mr Porter driving the horse and cart sedately towards St Benedicts and he would stop and let us rub the horse's nose amidst the tolerant traffic of the time.

One day, our choral exploits came to a bloody end, as the bench toppled over backwards and my brother and I each gashed all eight fingers as we hung on the rusty, corrugated top edge of the fence, our legs kicking wildly! My poor mother, confronted by both her bawling off-spring, their every finger dripping blood, had to rush round to Miss Brown's general stores for more Elastoplast, never having dreamt she would need sixteen at one go! I think she despaired of us, sometimes.

I know my father despaired of me. I broke more windows than anyone I have ever known, practising my beloved football. I was always taught that if I did something wrong, it would be better to own up, then the punishment wouldn't be so severe. Having just broken the third window of the fortnight, something told me it would be prudent to go and confess.

Father was dealing with a customer on the garage forecourt and I hovered around silently praying and chewing a penn'orth of Blackjacks from Miss Brown's. (That meant four at once, another misdemeanour – two at once was considered adequate.) When he noticed me, he broke off with the customer and listened while I moved the Blackjacks into my cheek pocket and blurted out my latest transgression. 'Alright.' he said quite calmly. 'I'll be round the back in a minute. Just wait for me there,' and turned back to his business. Relief flooded through me as I skipped back to the scene of the crime and rewarded myself for my good fortune with another four Blackjacks. I was on my twenty-third 'keepie-uppie' with 'Exhibit A', the football, when my father strode into view. He shouted and raved, gesticulated at the broken glass, yelled, roared and bellowed about my clumsiness and naughtiness and the cost of repeatedly replacing glass and finally taking hold of my shoulders, he began to shake me. Unseen by him as he shook me, my softened mound of Blackjacks executed a perfect arc from my mouth, landing on the bare earth, just under the wooden bench, (that of the earlier Elastoplast episode.) 'Go to your room and stay there!' he commanded. 'And don't come down for *Journey into Space*, either!'

This was a punishment of the first order. Deprived of Lemmy and the Gang's radio adventures at 7 p.m. I hoped my brother would listen and fill me in, but he had gone to a birthday tea and I didn't know what time he would be back. It was only 6 p.m, but I knew better than to argue. I trailed off discontentedly to my bedroom but at least I had a Famous Five to finish before tomorrow, when I would spend my penny bus-fare on a toffee-apple from Mrs Ladbroke, the milkman's wife, and instead walk down to Duke Street and the library. In the meantime, I contemplated my Blackjacks lying forlornly under the bench.

From the window of my parent's bedroom, it was possible to see the whole garage forecourt and things seemed to be quite normal out there. Old Bernard, who had worked here long before I was born, was checking an inner tube for punctures in an old bath full of filthy water and Father had just filled a car with petrol and was now checking its oil. I decided to chance it.

I was down the stairs in a trice, through the living-room and kitchen, then through the room we euphemistically called the 'Conservatory', (well, it did have a glass roof) past the wind-up gramophone and its little tin box of needles and our two records, Al Jolston's 'Sonny Boy' and Paul Robeson's 'Old Man River' and out into the garden.

Thankfully unheard and unseen, I approached my beloved Blackjacks, whose size appeared to have grown a hundred-fold! And actually they had, for I was now sharing them with most of the residents of a nearby ants' nest! Undeterred, I grabbed the Blackjacks up and rushed in to swill all the ants away under the kitchen tap. Satisfied it was now ant free, I popped it comfortingly back into my mouth and, chewing happily, darted back upstairs to finish the Famous Five's adventures!

By then, I was a pupil at Wensum View Junior School, on Turner Road and played in all the school and house netball and rounders teams. But football was still my first love and I spent all my spare time practising dribbling, trapping, passing and shooting footballs with my brother and anyone who would give a girl player the time of day. Grudgingly at first, but gradually more acceptingly, the boys would let me join their games. And the day that I was actually chosen to play, instead of having to be on one side or the other because I was the last unpicked player, I could have burst with pride. And I don't think I ever let them down, except maybe the day I jumped off a swing at its zenith on the little park on Dereham Road behind the school, severely hurting my arm. Nevertheless, I played the game, went home to dinner (lunch) and found I couldn't hold my knife. The subsequent visit to the hospital, x-ray and plaster up to my shoulder for six weeks was the upshot of both a broken wrist and elbow!

Not long after this, and in a uniform meant to last at least two years rather than fit, I started at the Blyth Grammar school at the top of Constitution Hill. I cycled to school everyday, played hockey and tennis there, but still loved football. I suppose my adolescent hormones were to blame, but I had the most enormous crush on Bobby Charlton. No Cliff or Elvis for me, although I will admit to an approximate six-month dalliance with Adam Faith, but basically I was 'Bobby's Girl'!

Two hundred and two photos of Mr Charlton bedecked my bedroom, the most prized even autographed! So, what then was a girl to do when suddenly in 1958 Norwich City embarked on their famous Cup run and discovered their third round opponents on Saturday 10 January 1959 were to be Manchester United and therefore the beloved Bobby?

I didn't actually support Man United as a team, I supported Norwich so that helped, but I felt very disloyal to Bobby the day that I purchased two yards each of yellow and green ribbon from Woolworth's and tied them to my prized brass bugle that always accompanied me to Carrow Road. Incidentally, I got the bus home from the city centre that afternoon, finding a seat upstairs. One of the windows was open and at intervals I proudly blew the bugle out of it, its yellow and green ribbons streaming nicely.

Next morning at school, before assembly I was asked by my form-mistress to go and stand outside the headmistress's office until I was called for. I was quickly summoned in and told to stand behind her enormous desk as she had something to say to me. After she lit a cigarette, (honestly!) and exhaled noisily once or twice, she began to relate how upset she had felt yesterday afternoon while in her car following a bus on Tombland and a pupil from this school had thought it sensible to blow a bugle out of a bus window!

I owned up, stating the mitigating circumstances that the whole city (bar one!) was enthralled by the prospect of the forthcoming match and accepted my punishment. 'Whatever possessed you?' she queried, giving me a detention. There was no answer that I could think of that would've been acceptable to an elderly, spinster headmistress.

Ticket fever now gripped the city. The only thing that anyone talked about was the prospect of getting tickets and huge queues formed at Carrow Road. Some of the lucky ones were pictured holding their tickets aloft in the *Eastern Evening News*. I knew I wouldn't be able to go, because playing truant to try and get tickets especially after the 'bus and bugle' episode didn't seem a good idea. I resigned myself to that and actually, I don't remember ever feeling jealous or upset. In those days we knew our boundaries and then just got on with life. But it didn't stop me dreaming…

The night before the match I had the most vivid dream. There was Matt Busby

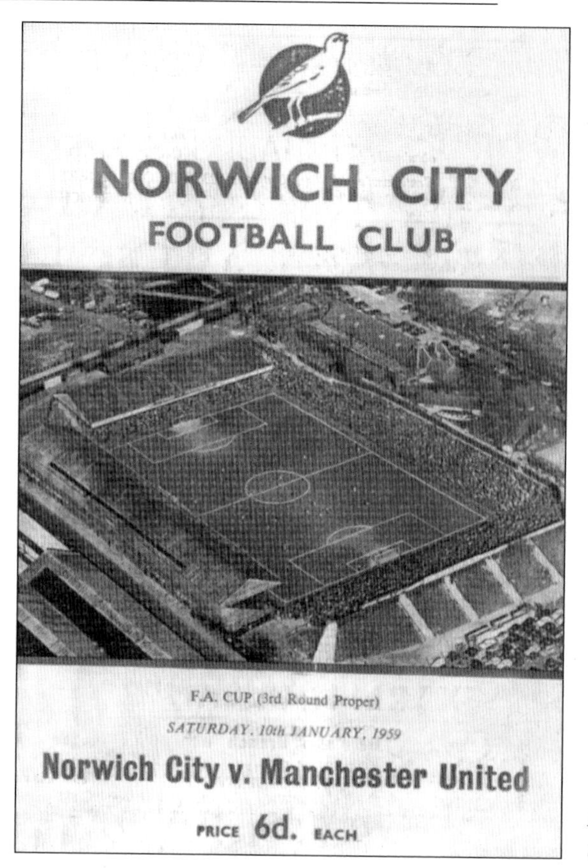

Programme for Norwich City vs Manchester Utd, 10 January 1969.

standing just outside one of the River End turnstiles calling for a volunteer to man it for some reason or another. I got the job and he passed me a sack and told me to tear each ticket in two as the queue passed through and drop them in the sack. Then he said, 'At three o'clock you will be allowed to dip into the sack and if you pull out two matching halves, you can go in!' I don't know what happened, as I woke up at that point! But when I woke, it was to find that Saturday 10 January 1959 had dawned icy-cold and snow covered. Oh, no! What if the match was postponed? I couldn't bear all this nervous anticipation again. So, well wrapped up, wellies on and a huge bowl of Mum's lovely porridge inside me, I set out on my bike for Carrow Road to ask if they needed any help in clearing the pitch?

In those days things were different. Mothers wouldn't be worried about young girls biking off unescorted to football grounds on the other side of the city and football clubs welcomed all visitors without security. So, there I was, a chubby, red-faced twelve-and-a-half-year-old girl who had just left her bike propped up outside the Main Entrance to Carrow Road, without a lock and who was now striding purposefully into the area just inside. I looked around me for a moment, wondering where to go, when a tall gentleman dressed very smartly in a suit and open overcoat came up to me. 'Hello?' he said questioningly. 'Hello,' I replied. 'Er, I was just wondering if you needed anyone else to help clear the pitch? I mean, with all this snow…'

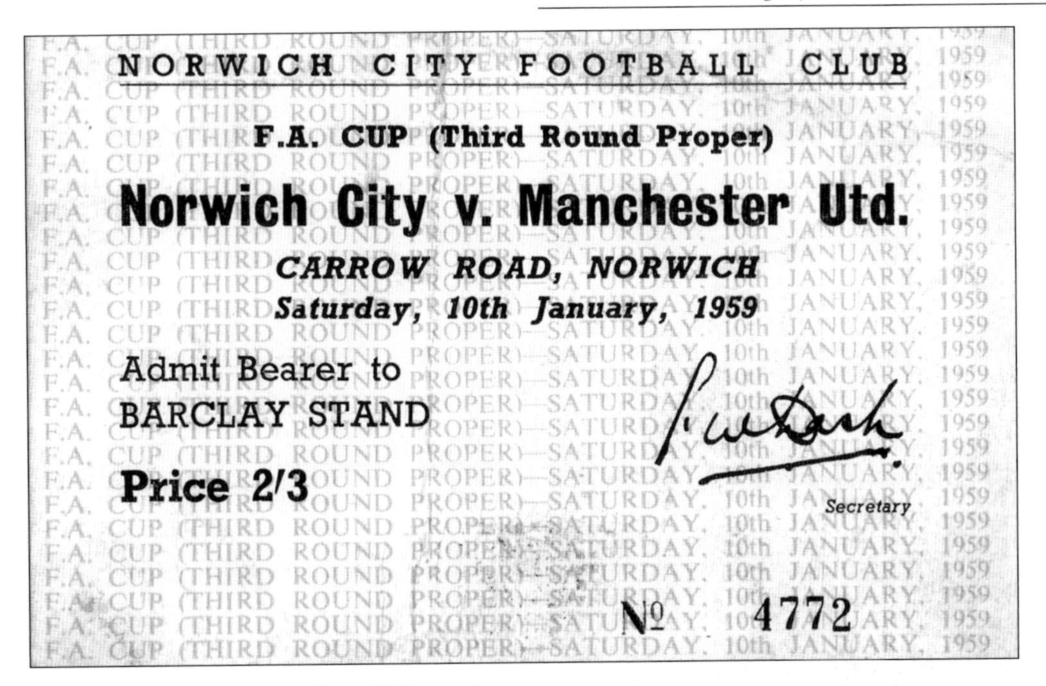
NORWICH CITY FOOTBALL CLUB

F.A. CUP (Third Round Proper)

Norwich City v. Manchester Utd.

CARROW ROAD, NORWICH

Saturday, 10th January, 1959

Admit Bearer to

BARCLAY STAND

Price 2/3

Secretary

№ 4772

Ticket for the match against Manchester Utd.

'That's very kind of you,' he said, ' but I think it's all under control.' 'So the match won't be cancelled?' 'Not unless things get very much worse and I don't think they will,' he smiled. 'Are you coming this afternoon?' 'No, afraid not, I was at school when the tickets were on sale. But I really hope they win!' I said fervently, with silent apologies to R. Charlton Esq.

And this is the stuff of dreams. This gentleman, who I assume was connected in some way with the management of Norwich City Football Club, held his suit lapel forward, withdrew a wallet from his inside pocket, opened it and handed me a ticket! 'So do I! Enjoy the game,' he said and with a small wave he turned and left, leaving me calling out my disbelieving thanks to his retreating back. It was as if my bike had sprouted wings as I flew home through the snowy streets to share my unbelievable good-fortune with my mum.

I had to go straight back and start to queue. It was quarter to one, sunny, yet very cold and ages yet before they would open the gates. Mum had put me some lemon-curd sandwiches in a paper bag and made sure I wore an extra pair of socks, but I remember shivering as I waited to rush in and bag my favourite spot behind and just to the right of the River End goal.

The rest, as they say, is history, local history, local folklore. The lad from Litcham, Terry Bly, grabbed the individual headlines after scoring twice and making the third, but there clearly was only one team in it – Norwich City! How the mighty (Utd) were fallen!

As the 38,000 ecstatic supporters poured out of the ground around a quarter to five, I, as one of the smallest, was borne along Carrow Road and into Riverside Road by the press of the crowd, my feet totally off the ground! 'On the ball, City', we roared! For the second time that day I was flying!

Diane de Rees

Kathleen Rogers at Cley Mill, 1946.

Cream teas and mud pies!

It was 1946 and the war, thankfully, was over. My husband, Bob, had finished his overseas service of four years in the Middle East and India. He was a regular in the Royal Air Force and he was posted to Langham near the coast of north Norfolk, in East Anglia. I lived at that time in Norwich with my grandmother, which had been my home since I was born.

Bob found the countryside surrounding Langham enchanting and fell in love with it, especially with Blakeney on the coast. The year 1946 was a good one for the weather, especially the summer, which was very warm and dry and so my husband suggested we spend as much time as possible at the weekends at the coast. Unfortunately, I was unable to live in married quarters at Langham, as none were available, and anyway, I was working in Norwich.

One Sunday, we decided to ask two people we had met casually in a pub to come in our

Kathleen Rogers boating at Morston, 1946.

car with us to the coast. The young lady and fellow were delighted and we proceeded on our way. We stopped at an 'Olde Worlde' inn and began chatting to the landlord who advised us to go to Morston, where we could be rowed over to the nature reserve on Blakeney Point. (Prince Charles visited this lovely place recently, in 1996.)

We found Morston and a genial boatman rowed us over to our destination, which to our delight appeared the most marvellous place. The sea, a deep blue, shimmered beneath the hot summer sun, whilst seals twisted and turned, playing in the gentle waves. There were many species of birds I had never seen before and all kinds of wild flowers and grasses growing in profusion. It was indeed an idyllic place.

Early in the afternoon we found a quaint little café that looked as though it was propped up on stilts. There we ate scones, with lots of cream and had a big pot of tea. After this, we decided to find the boatman and return to Morston, which we did, but when alighting from the boat we all slithered one by one and fell on our posteriors in the awful slushy mess of seaweed, sand and goodness knows what else! The two men had slushy mud all over their smart new post-war trousers and we two females found our frocks were in a shocking state. We went behind some bushes to remove our knickers and nylons, because they felt claggy and awful! It was impossible to sit in the car, in such a mess, all the way back to Norwich! Bob had to drive back with bare feet, which was most uncomfortable.

On the way back we stopped at the inn we had visited in the morning, where we were greeted with guffaws of laughter from the yokels, one of whom said, 'Cor bor, what a rum do, wherever you bin to git in that thar state?' We all joined in the laughter!

However, the episode didn't deter Bob and me from going again; but when we did we wore shorts and plimsolls and just in case catastrophe struck again we took a change of underwear! Incidentally, our new friends didn't contact us again. (I wonder why?) Maybe it wasn't their idea of a pleasant day out, even though they had laughed at the spectacle we made covered in slushy slime from the North Sea!

Kathleen Rogers

Queen Victoria's Golden Jubilee, 1887

There is nothing the people of Norwich like more than a royal spectacle, as this photograph from 1887 shows. It is not surprising in a way that the people were so excited, as Norwich had not been visited by a reigning monarch for 216 years, since Charles II came in 1671, and no other would come until Edward VII in 1909. It was Edward VII who made Norfolk a royal county once more as he based himself at Sandringham during his time as Prince of Wales. Since 1909 there have been many royal visits and they have all received the same level of excitement as the Golden Jubilee of 1887.

Sarah Skinner

Norwich celebrates Queen Victoria's Golden Jubilee in 1887.

A picture postcard montage of Sandringham views.

Contributors' Biographies

So that these amazing memories were not just credited to faceless names, we asked the authors of the pieces selected to supply a little bit of information and a photograph where possible.

Monica Olwen Bowling
(Playplaces of our childhood)
She has lived mostly in Norwich since August 1916 (apart from a wide gap), and describes herself as a housewife. She says, 'I have bought a tiny eighteenth-century cottage, hidden away in the little known corner of 'Norwich-over-the-water'. It is within a stone's throw of my father's old Presbyterian school and the schoolhouse at St Augustine's, where I was born – both long since reduced to dust. Here, surrounded by my past, as my mind's eye sees in photographic detail the city I once knew; and my mind's ear hears the old cadences: speech patterns and double-negatives of the beloved Norfolk accent (now subsumed in homogeneous Estuary English). I fill my hours with writing – poetry, stories and letters.'

Monica Bowling.

Jack Burton.

Molly Burton.

Barbara Brown
(Wroxham Village School, Spartan holidays in Brundall)
She lives in Coulsdon, Surrey, and retired early from a Data Centre.
She has fond memories of when she lived in Wroxham, with a dyke at the end of the garden. Her father was evacuated to the area during the First World War and subsequently brought his family here later on.

Wesley Bullen
(Building blocks of the past)
He has lived in Ditchingham for fifty-five years and is now retired. He was born on 7 November 1919 to Primitive Methodists and went to Bungay Grammar School, leaving in 1936 to take up a clerical position. Called up in 1940, he served in Africa, Italy and Germany, met a German girl in Hamburg and later married her back in the UK. He worked at Clays the printers until retirement in 1984. He has celebrated his fifty-fifth wedding anniversary and has grown-up children and grandchildren.

Jack Burton
(Colegate – the street of light)
He has lived in Norwich more or less since his birth in 1939. He is a bus driver for Eastern Counties Buses and also a Methodist Minister. He says 'There is no better place to

Michael Crouch.

Andrew Daniels.

live than Norwich'. He writes a regular column for the *Eastern Daily Press* and served as Sheriff of Norwich in 1988.

Molly Burton
(Sunday school treats)
She has lived in Norwich for thirty-four years and is a housewife, moving to Norwich when she married. She is a keen gardener and football fan and holds a season ticket to Carrow Road.

Michael Crouch
(St Andrew's Hall)
He has lived in Norwich all his life (thirty-seven years) and is an eRecords Designer for BT. He lives in Norwich, as it is 'a good-looking city with plenty for everyone'. He has spent a few years digging into family history and local history and has put all of this together in his own web site.

Andrew Daniels
(Argyle Street in the 1950s)
He was brought up in Norwich and although he has lived in a variety of places he has spent most of his life here. He is currently an art history researcher. He wishes to thank his son for prompting him to write the article declares he has 'enjoyed applying his mind to the subject.'

Sue Debbage.

Daphne Dennis

Sue Debbage
(Hilda's war)

She has lived in Norwich for thirty years and works as a warden at the Friend's Meeting House. She lives in Norwich because of 'roots, beauty, history – where else?' Hilda is her (ex) mother-in-law and, although now in frail physical health, has memories that are strong and fresh. The family have all heard her stories over the years and will be happy to share her memories with others. Sue recorded the interviews as an Open University project and hopes to have further articles published in the *Norfolk Archaeologists and Historical Research Journal.*

Daphne Dennis
(A Family United through War and Peace)

She has lived in Norwich most of her life and is married to Ken, a retired Police Sergeant. They had two children: Andrew, now living and working in Zurich, and Tracey, who they lost in 1993 after a long illness. Daphne has had a variety of jobs, including telephonist at the Norwich telephone exchange and Norfolk News Company and medical receptionist at Thorpe Health Centre and Thorpe Veterinary Clinic. Among her main interests now is her charity work for Age Concern and the Copper Atkinson Trust, the latter being a local charity that helps Indian street children.

Diane de Rees.

Diane de Rees
(How the mighty (Utd) were fallen!)
She has lived in Norwich all her life and is a mature student. Norwich is 'her home, her roots and her heart'. She knows Norfolk well through a variety of jobs including mobile librarian, Post Office assistant and owner of a tourist shop on the Broads.

John Ferguson
(Late Victorian matriarchs)
He has lived in Norwich, off and on, all of his life and is a retired social work manager. He lives in Norwich as it is a 'fine city'. He wishes 'more shops would run competitions to encourage new writing. The advantage of writing as a hobby is that, unlike most, minimal equipment is required.'

Jenny Fox
(The reign of Black Anna)
She works as a nursing sister at Saxlingham Hall Nursing Home and enjoys writing, reading, walking and travelling. She has travelled extensively has settled in Norwich, finding it a pleasant place to live – 'It caters for all age groups while maintaining its individuality and I have no plans to leave.' She would like to credit Mrs Theresa Parfitt of Bergh Apton for her patience and computer skills while compiling the piece, the Forum Heritage Library for their help and

Josephine Jenkins.

Evelyn Knights.

assistance, and the *Eastern Daily Press* for their articles and reference material.

Valerie Harley
(Not all doom and gloom)
She has lived in Norwich for seventy-three years. 'I am here because it is where all my family is and because it is such a nice place to live.'

Josephine Jenkins
(Four paintings and a Life Room past)
She has lived in Norwich for three years and is a freelance artist. She originally moved to the city to study and likes living here as 'the city has lots of character.'

Evelyn Knights
(Bonds and bombs)
She was a nurse during the Second World War and kindly supplied us with photographs of herself both then and now.

Sandra Massen
(A village childhood)
She has lived in Norwich for thirty-two years and is a shop assistant in a local newsagents and says that she lives in Norwich as 'it is such a pleasant place to live'.

Kathleen Rogers
(Cream teas and mud pies)
She was born in Norwich and returned to

Kathleen Rogers.

Valerie Turner.

live here to be close to her daughter when she retired four years ago. She has fond memories of life here before and during the war working in various jobs around the city but although so much has changed, this area is still so beautiful that she was very pleased to return.

Valerie Turner
(Wartime Christmas happiness)
She has lived in Norwich all her life and is a recently retired teacher. She says, 'The word 'awkward' is sometimes used to describe people round here but whatever the chosen description I'm proud to be an East Anglian!'

Raymond Vincent
(A city childhood, A working city through young eyes)
After being given an old computer by his grandson Peter Chenery (who submitted these pieces on Raymond's behalf), he wrote a stream of articles for his local parish magazine and started to compile memoirs of his life. These two pieces were parts of different articles and show the level of detail of his memories and the liveliness of his work.

Anthony Ward
('Play that ol' piana')
He has lived in Norwich all his life (seventy-

Anthony Ward.

Peter Warrington.

three years) and is a retired piano maker and tuner. He spent some time as a steward on British coastal ships before returning to Norwich to marry and raise a family.

Peter Warrington
(The Cathedral church of St John the Baptist)
He moved to Norwich for a job in the Civil Service twenty-six years ago and stayed. He is now retired and he and his wife have been involved in parish activities at St Johns for many years. He is a Cathedral guide and his wife a member of the Cathedral flower-arranging team.